JONAH'S

Emotional

JOURNEY

By

Dennis W. Jackson, M. Div., D.D.S.

DEDICATION

This book is dedicated with love to the following:

To my wife, *Stephanie*, you have truly inspired me to become a better person. I cannot believe how blessed I am to be with you.

To my two awesome kids, *Drew and Starr*, it is my greatest privilege to be a part of your lives.

To my parents, *Robert and Alice Hobbs*, your wisdom and example in my life have been unparalleled.

To my sisters, *Felicia Flora and Gayle Womack-El*, we have worked together, and we have shared some of the best times together.

To all of us who struggle with emotions along life's journey.

CONTENTS

ACKNOWLEDGEMENTS

With very special thanks:

* To my wife, ***Stephanie***, for her love, advice, feedback, and encouragement. When I did not think I could do it, she knew I could.

* To my sister, ***Felicia Flora***, for her years of dedication and support in the dental office.

* To my sister, ***Gayle Womack-El***, whose insight, editing, and vision turned this series of sermons into a book.

* To my kids, ***Drew and Starr***, who give me hope for the future.

* To my parents, ***Robert and Alice Hobbs***, for laying the foundation for the to take this journey of discovery.

* To my dental staff, ***Lynelle and Melissa***, whose patience allowed me to pursue this ambition.

INTRODUCTION

In 2006, while seeking the Lord for a sermon to write, the Lord directed me to read the *Book of Jonah*. I had read this book at least once before, and I had heard several sermons on the subject. However, the sermons I had heard were all basically the same: Jonah was in the belly of the whale for three days, as Christ was in the grave for three days. The fish then spit Jonah up onto dry land, and he went on to save the city of Nineveh, just as Christ rose from the grave and went on to save humanity.

As a result of those past experiences, I did not expect to discover anything different upon reading the Book of Jonah this time. Therefore, I read Jonah and nothing happened. Then, the Lord led me to read the *Book of Jonah* a second time and, still, I saw nothing new. However, the Lord directed me to read *Jonah* a third time, and then the book opened up for me – Jonah had been on an emotional journey.

Yes, Jonah went to the seaport at Joppa to board a ship headed across the sea to Tarshish.

Yet, at the same time, Jonah was embarking on an emotional expedition. He journeyed to the ports of embarrassment, guilt, depression, suicide, grief, and anger.

I was amazed to discover that, in my lifetime, I had been making this same emotional voyage. In fact, I believe we all have traveled to and spent time in these emotional ports of call. Maybe, you have not considered suicide, but I know you have been angry. Perhaps, you have never dealt with depression, but I am sure you have experienced embarrassment. And who among us has not known guilt or grief?

Therefore, I invite you to join me aboard Jonah's ship of emotional discovery. Let us see what the Lord has to teach us about navigating the seas of life's emotional journey.

CHAPTER 1

CALL ON GOD

EXPLORING THE EMOTION OF EMBARRASSMENT

Now the word of the LORD came unto Jonah the son of Amittai, saying, 2) Arise, go to Nineveh, that great city, and cry against it; for their wickedness is come up before me. 3) But Jonah rose up to flee unto Tarshish from the presence of the LORD, and went down to Joppa; and he found a ship going to Tarshish: so he paid the fare therof, and went down into it, to go with them unto Tarshish from the presence of the LORD. 4) But the LORD sent out a great wind into the sea, and there was a mighty tempest in the sea, so that the ship was like to be broken. 5) Then the mariners were afraid, and cried every man unto his god, and cast forth the wares that were in the ship into the sea, to lighten it of them. But Jonah was gone down into the sides of the ship; and he lay, and was fast asleep. 6) So the shipmaster came to him, and said unto him, What meanest thou, O sleeper? Arise, call upon thy God, if so be that God will think upon us, that we perish not. Jonah 1:1-6

The word of the Lord came to Jonah telling him to go to Nineveh, that great city, and cry against it because their wickedness had come up before God. Nineveh, at the time, was a metropolis of the Assyrian (now Iraq) monarchy. A sizeable city, it encompassed an area of over 48 miles with a great number of inhabitants approximating over one million people, making Nineveh larger than the city of Babylon.

The city of Nineveh was great in that it was powerful, wealthy, and influential. Yet, Nineveh was a heathen or wicked city, one that neither revered nor worshipped the true and living God. And its inhabitants had sinned so much and to such a degree that it could no longer be ignored or glossed over. Something had to be done.

RUNNING AWAY

Parents, you know all about this type of behavior. You'll tell your child not to eat any candy until after he's had his dinner, but he goes on and eats it anyway. Or perhaps you, a non-smoker, have company over whom you tell not to smoke in your house, but they smoke anyway. This is how the people of Nineveh behaved. They blatantly sinned against God right in His face without any attempt to hide it.

Therefore, God told Jonah to cry against the city of Nineveh and to do it quickly. Do not wait. Do not delay. Go quickly. Warn the city of Nineveh of the destruction that was coming if it did not change its evil ways. ***But Jonah rose up to flee unto Tarshish from the presence of the LORD… (Jonah 1:3).*** Wow! Jonah heard God's word, and then he went in the *opposite* direction. Nineveh was inland toward the east, and Tarshish was on the coast of Spain across the sea in the west.

Now, I do not know about you, but it drives me crazy when I tell one of my kids to come here, and he runs away, or when I tell one of them to listen to me, and she keeps on talking. If you say look at this and instead your child looks away, it can really drive you crazy, right? When you tell one of your kids to do something and he or she does the exact opposite, it can make you feel, I don't know, disrespected.

You may find yourself asking questions like, "Am I speaking out loud? I mean, I feel my lips moving, but is any sound coming out? Can they hear me? Maybe they cannot see me. Hello? Hello?" Most of us like it when people at least pretend to pay attention to what we are saying, especially if we're in a position of authority, for example: a parent with a child, a teacher with a student, or a boss with an employee.

I had been a dentist in private practice for years and, at one time, I decided to purchase a second dental office. I thought it would be a good idea to keep the staff that had been working there for years for the former owner. I told them that we were going to do things a little differently than how they were done under their former employer.

One particular assistant, however, just could not seem to adjust to the few changes I had made. I would tell her that we were going to do a procedure in a certain way. She would look me straight in the eyes and say, "Okay, Dr. Jackson, we'll do it just like you want it done." Then, sure enough, she would do it just as she had always done it before. This went on for about three weeks – me telling her to do something, her agreeing to do it as I had asked, then her doing it the way she wanted. So, I fired her. I just could not see paying someone who openly ignored or defied me.

The truth is when we talk to someone, we want that person to listen and respond. He should at least act like he's trying to comply and not take off running in the opposite direction. It makes us feel completely disrespected. So imagine how God must have felt. God knew that Jonah had heard His voice.

Jonah was a prophet, a man hand-picked by God to hear and deliver God's word to His people. Yet, Jonah chose not to listen to God's word – the same word that made heaven and earth, the same word that cannot return void, the same word that must accomplish whatever God sends it out to accomplish.

However, it is easy for us to point the finger at Jonah. We hear the word of God preached to us and we read the written word of God in our Bibles. Still, how many of us really do *all* that the word of God tells us to do? Most of us act like Jonah. Though we hear the word of God come forth to us on Sunday morning, we spend the rest of the week running in the opposite direction.

You may think that it just is not cool to do what God's word tells you to do. You may feel like a stupid fool to forgive someone who hurt you. You may feel it's dumb to love your enemies simply because God first loved you. You may feel you couldn't imagine feeding, clothing or helping someone who is out to get you. But that is exactly what God's word tells us to do.

You may even find it boring not to cheat, steal, lie, or get drunk or high so that you can keep your body as God's temple and His living sacrifice. And it certainly seems absurd to only have sex when you're married. After all, you wouldn't even buy a car that you didn't first take out for a test drive.

Anyway, half of all marriages break up, so why go through all the trouble of making it legal? You'll stay together as long as you're feeling it. Then, when you stop feeling it, you will just end the relationship, right?

Besides, it seems like the word of God made more sense for our parents in their time than it does for us today. We no longer phone; we text. We no longer pay cash; we use credit. We no longer go to church; we watch church on TV. But God's word still works. God's word made heaven and earth, and it is still effective today. God's word saves you and me. God's word will never lose its power. God's word is the key to living a life of victory.

WHAT WILL OTHERS THINK OF ME?

The truth is I do believe that Jonah respected God. And, although Jonah was disobedient, I believe that he disobeyed God because he felt he had a good reason. As he expressed to God in

Chapter 4 verse 2 *...I pray thee, O LORD, was not this my saying, when I was yet in my country? Therefore I fled before unto Tarshish: for I knew that thou art a gracious God, and merciful, slow to anger, and of great kindness, and repentest thee of the evil.* In other words, Jonah did not want to go to Nineveh, that great city, and cry against it with a warning of coming judgment and destruction, only for God not to follow through with it. Jonah did not want to look bad. He did not want to be embarrassed.

Some Bible scholars say that Jonah was worried about his safety. See, Nineveh was a big city like New York City, Philadelphia, Chicago, Albuquerque, or Los Angeles. So, scholars think Jonah feared that after he delivered such a stern message of correction from God to the people of Nineveh, they would openly defy God, take out their frustration on him, and maybe even kill him.

It certainly is possible that the people of Nineveh would have beaten and killed Jonah. Yet, as seen in Chapter 4 verse 2, Jonah did not mention that he fled because he had been afraid for his life. No he did not. More likely, Jonah felt that if he were to cry out and prophesy death and destruction to the people of Nineveh, God would forgive them and nothing would happen. If God did forgive

Nineveh and spare its people, Jonah felt he would be thought of as just another false prophet.

If nothing happened after he had cried out and prophesied to the people, Jonah felt he would be regarded as just another nut, and the city is chock full of them. Didn't some kook just predict that the world would end exactly on Saturday, May 21, 2011?! Jonah simply did not want to become another screw loose in the machine of the big city. He did not want to look bad. Jonah simply did not want to be embarrassed.

LOOKING OUT FOR NUMBER ONE

Certain Bible scholars support that Jonah tried to run away from his God-given commission to prophesy to Nineveh because of his own racial bias. They feel that Jonah fled because he did not want the people of Nineveh to be saved. After all, Jonah knew that God had spared the children of Israel countless times before. For example, when Aaron yielded to the complaints of the children of Israel and fashioned a golden calf for them to worship while Moses was atop Mt. Sinai receiving the Ten Commandments, God did punish many of them for their sin of idol worship. Yet, most of them He spared. Jonah may have worried that God had finally had enough of the children of Israel's disobedience and was going to replace them with the people of Nineveh.

Admittedly, it is quite possible that Jonah did not want Nineveh to be spared because the people were not the "right" color, class, or religion. After all, Jonah was the first prophet to be sent to the Gentiles, much like Apostles Peter and Paul would be sent many years later. However, people generally tend to operate based on how matters affect them personally. The truth is most people are a little self-centered.

Yes, there are definitely those who are concerned about the big picture. Martin Luther King, Jr., Mother Teresa, and John f. Kennedy come to mind as having been genuinely concerned about people, cultures, and countries. To the opposite extreme, Hitler and Osama Bin Laden focused on the "big picture" but in the most negative and detrimental of ways. However, most who claim to be concerned about others, their families, or their well-being actually are looking out for number one – self.

Take politicians, for example. I am suspicious of any politician who wants to cut Medicare and Social Security benefits, for which senior citizens worked all their lives or depend on for daily living, but refuses to cut subsidies to the *multi-BILLION* dollar oil companies, which are making record profits. I am also suspicious of any car sales person who says he is concerned about me and my family being safe and comfy in a particular car, van or SUV. Do I think that he really cares about me or my family? No. He just met me, so how could he care? What he cares about is me buying that car, van or SUV so he can get the commission to feed his own family.

So, I may sound cynical, but I just cannot help but think that Jonah's reasons for taking such a huge risk and being disobedient to God's word were personal. The Prophet Jonah simply did not want to be embarrassed or to look bad. And while his reasons for disobeying God's word may have been a combination of all three – concern for his safety, racial bias, and fear of embarrassment – they all boil down to Jonah looking out for himself.

AVOIDING THE SPOTLIGHT

Look at it this way. If Jonah had gone to Nineveh and prophesied that God would destroy the city and God actually did it, then Jonah's popularity would have exploded. Jonah would have been considered the number one prophet in the country. Jonah would have made it onto day time television and talk radio and would have been featured on the cover of Newsweek and

10

Time Magazines (metaphorically speaking, of course). But because Jonah believed that the people of Nineveh would repent and that God would spare them, he feared he would look like a false prophet and be mortified. Therefore, Jonah thought, "Why, bother? Why risk messing up my reputation? I'll just play it safe and avoid the whole scene all together."

The truth is no one likes to be embarrassed. No one wants to look bad. This is what stage fright is all about: people shying away from acting, preaching, or singing in public to avoid everyone looking at them and to avoid everyone knowing if they were to mess up.   The contestants on *American Idol, Dancing with the Stars,* and *So You Think You Can Dance,* for example, are well aware of the risks of being in the spotlight. They know that millions of people are watching them, critiquing them, and may even be laughing at them. But for them, embarrassment is a chance they are willing to take for a shot at fifteen minutes of fame. For Jonah, however, it simply was not. He chose not to put himself out there for public display and possible humiliation.

I have had my share of humiliating moments in public, so I understand how Jonah may have felt. Once, I was singing the lead to a song for my church choir.

I remember just singing away, happy as could be that they had chosen me to be the lead singer, when suddenly someone yelled out, "Dennis, you are singing the *wrong words*!" How embarrassing was that? In fact, that is why, to this day, I carry my notebook to the pulpit whenever I preach. If I do forget what I am supposed to say, I can quickly refer to my notes and avoid making that mistake again.

As another example, one year, I decided to do some dental health spots on the radio. I am sure you have heard these radio spots: The radio host chats with the dentist for a few minutes about dentistry; the dentist takes a few calls and answers a few questions from the radio audience; he (or she) then does his best to encourage the listeners to come to his dental office for any further consultation and eventual treatment. I figured doing this would be good advertisement for my dental practice and would bring in more business.

So I agreed to be on the *Rev. Russell Fox Gospel Radio Show*. I told everyone I knew that I would be on the *Rev. Russell Fox Gospel Radio Show*. My wife and kids, my family and friends, and even my accountant promised to listen to me on the *Rev. Russell Fox Gospel Radio Show*.

Anyway, while I was driving to the radio station that morning, I was listening to *another* radio show. The host of that radio show was the *Rev. Dell Shields*. So, when I got on the air, the host of the radio show that I was on – Rev. Russell Fox – said, "Hi, Dr. Jackson." And I said, "Hi, Rev. SHIELDS." I called him the *WRONG NAME*! Suddenly, I realized that I had called the host, Rev. Russell Fox, by the other radio host's name. So, I said, "I am sorry, Rev. Shields. I meant to say *Rev. SHIELDS*". I had brain lock. I just could not stop calling the host, Rev. Fox, by the name, Rev. Shields.

Even though the radio station was cold, all of a sudden it got hot. Beads of sweat started popping out of my forehead, and time seemed to stop. My mouth got dry. And I could actually feel my heart beating in my chest – thump-thump, thump-thump – and this all happened live on the air! Everybody I knew was listening. Finally, the host said, "My name is *Rev. Russell Fox*." I wanted to run and hide. I wanted to disappear. I felt *so embarrassed*......

I think that we all have been embarrassed at one time or another. Remember when you were a child, and someone would pull a prank or play a trick on you? Let's say, you were about to sit down and somebody would pull the chair out

13

from under you. Everybody in the class would have a big laugh, but it would not be at all funny to you. To you, it would feel demeaning.

And as kids reach teen age, they often become embarrassed by their parents. At age thirteen, many teenagers will no longer let their mothers kiss them in public. Some thirteen year-olds will go as far as telling their parent who drove them to school to drop them off a block away from school just so they can act like they walked there themselves. Some teens may even feel ashamed to be seen with their parents in public for fear that their peers may find their parents too poor, uncouth, or un-cool.

Ironically, parents often feel the same way about their children. I cannot count how many times my mother, when she had company come over or saw someone she thought was important, would say to me, "Sit up straight, act like you have some sense, and do not embarrass me." Parents do tend to take

Whatever, their children do as a personal reflection on them. If a child were getting good grades in school, playing well in sports, married with a baby, or faring well in life, then the parents would brag on him or her and tell anyone who would listen. But if that same child were struggling in school, struggling in life, or struggling with an addiction, then they would not even mention their child because they would consider him or her a disgrace.

We also become embarrassed over money matters. Have you ever had a sales clerk take your credit card away and destroy it? Or has a cashier ever told you that you may not use your card and asked, "Do you have another means of payment?" Of course, scenes like this only seem to happen when there is a long line of customers waiting behind you, staring right at you.

Being seen not looking your best can make you feel self-conscious as well. Have you ever run out to the grocery store dressed in a holey tee shirt, sweat pants, and house shoes because it's late at night, all you need is a light bulb, bread or some juice for the kids, and you figure, "No one important will see me anyway?" Sure enough, that is when you see a co-worker, a church member, your boss, your pastor, or someone you want to look your best around. So, what do you do? You try to hide between the aisles and hope they will leave the store without spotting you, so you won't feel so awkward.

I believe that is what Jonah was trying to do. Jonah wanted to avoid public humiliation so much that he figured hiding from God's presence was his only guarantee. So Jonah fled. He went to the seaport at Joppa and boarded a cargo ship that was headed across the sea in the opposite direction to the city of Tarshish in Spain. He wanted to get as far away as he possibly could from Nineveh to steer clear of any potential embarrassment.

WAKE UP, AND CALL ON GOD

So, Jonah thought all he had to do to avoid his God-given assignment and possible shame was to pay the fare and board the ship. Isn't it funny that when you want to do something wrong, it seems so easy, especially in the beginning? The first time you cheat, steal, or lie, you seem to get away with it. The first time you smoke, drink, or get high, it appears fun and exciting and that nothing bad will happen. Often, your buddies are even there egging you on; and, although it's a little scary, usually it goes fine.

Whether it is drinking, smoking, doing drugs, watching pornography, gambling, stealing, fornicating, or cheating on your spouse, the very first time you do it, it feels so exhilarating and you usually don't get caught. So, you say to yourself, "That was not so bad. Actually, it was fun and easy." However, you should know not to trust that feeling. In fact, just keep on doing whatever wrong it is that you are doing, and sooner or later, a storm will come and you will get caught out there in that storm.

That is exactly what happened to Jonah. Jonah thought that he was safe disobeying God. He actually thought that he was safe in his sin. So, after he had paid the fare and boarded the ship, he found a spot and went to sleep. Jonah figured he had made his escape. He thought God was not paying any attention, so he could just relax and take it easy. But the Lord sent a great wind. The Lord literally hurled a great wind into the sea at Jonah. This wind caused a storm so strong that the ship was in danger of being broken in two.

When you sin, ignore, and disobey God, sooner or later, I guarantee that God will send or allow a storm to rise up in your life. Then, it will seem like everyone and everything you care about will be tossed to and fro and almost broken in two. In fact, the storm will be so great that those in the ship of life with you – your family, friends, and co-workers – will wonder what is wrong. Your loved ones will find it especially strange when they look around the sea and notice that it appears calm for everyone else but you.

One translation of the Bible says that the storm only troubled the ship that Jonah was on. That means that for every other ship on the sea at that time, the sea was calm. The shipmates of your life, like your kids, for example, will see that everything or everyone else around you looks calm. And they'll say things like, "What is wrong with our family? Why can't we be normal? Why can't we be like everybody else?"

Chapter 1 verse 5a says, ***The mariners [or sailors] were afraid, and cried every man unto his god, and cast forth the wares [or cargo] that were in the ship into the sea, to lighten it of them…*** Keep in mind that it was a cargo ship that Jonah had boarded. But the mariners were so afraid for their lives that they cast their valuable cargo away. Even though the mariners had planned to make money by selling their cargo in Tarshish, they cast their goods into the sea in an attempt to steady the ship. After all, what good would money have been if they were to lose their lives?

The sailors thought that they could rescue themselves from the storm, and so will your family when they see they've been caught in the tempest with you. They will attempt to self-medicate with drugs, alcohol, and toxic relationships all in an effort to escape the storm or right the family ship. They may even let things go, like their behavior – getting into trouble in or out of school – or, their looks –becoming over weight or anorexic – all in attempt to lighten their emotional load. Any parent who has ever been divorced, for example, knows that the kids tend to blame themselves for their family's troubles. And then, they fling away things that used to matter to them, like their grades or positive peers.

Chapter 1 verse 6 says...***The shipmaster came to him, and said unto him, What meanest thou, O sleeper? Arise, call upon thy God, if so be that God will think upon us, that we perish not.*** In essence, the captain of the ship was questioning Jonah, "How can you be asleep at a time like this? Can't you see what is happening to everyone and everything around you? You cannot possibly be that obtuse, that unaware of the storm that we are all battling. Wake up! Get up! Get it together! Call on God! You have to get involved in saving this ship that you're on."

And that is what this passage of scripture is saying to those who have been caught out in the storm. "Pray. Call on God. Do whatever you have to do to save your job, your career, your marriage, or your family. Can't you see all is about to be lost, and you are lying there asleep?!

Stop pretending that nothing is wrong. Stop convincing your self that things are not so bad." What do people who are in denial often say? "Sure, everything is not perfect, but I know people who have it worse than we do. Plus, nobody really cares; nobody is watching or paying any attention to us." But if you are thinking this way, then you are wrong. God cares. God knows and sees all that you are going through. God is watching, and He will send a shipmaster to awaken you. God will send someone to challenge you, someone to question you and to ask you, "What is going on? What are you doing? Is sleeping through the storm really working for you?"

Someone will encourage you to wake up, and call on God. Do not delay; call on God. Do not ignore the storm; call on God. When nothing else has helped, call on God. Let's face it; if you already feel like all is lost, then what else have you got to lose? Call on God. He will not let you go down with the ship. He will not embarrass you. He wants to save, heal, and deliver you.

How sad, to think that the storm and all of the panic, loss and chaos that ensued came simply because Jonah did not want to be embarrassed. Yet, God is so loving, so kind, and so patient that, despite Jonah's disobedience, He sent the shipmaster to awaken Jonah. How ironic that the Prophet Jonah, who should have been waking and warning the city of Nineveh, had to be awakened and warned by someone whom he did not know and that did not know His God.

Yet, as children of God, this is precisely our job. Whether pastors, ministers, or lay people, we all can offer to someone, whose ship is being tossed to and fro, a chance to wake up and call on God.

In fact, anytime we see someone in trouble, whether we know that person well or not, we can pray for him or her and direct him or her to call on God. Remember, we are all in the ship of life together. We all can pray for our country, our states, our cities, our communities, our families, and our friends. And we certainly can pray for ourselves.

I do believe that prayer changes things. No matter how bad your situation might be and no matter how severe the storm in your life, God is just a prayer away. As long as you are alive and your ship is afloat, there is still time to pray. There is still hope.

Call on God. He hears your prayers and will not turn away. And when God hears your prayers and when He thinks on you, He will act on your behalf and deliver you.

Friend, do not continue to go your own way. Call on God to be set on the path to victory. Call on God to be alcohol and drug free. Call on God to be financially free. Call on God, so you will not perish. Call on God, so your marriage will flourish. Call on God. He is waiting on you. Call on God. He will not embarrass you. Call on God. He will see you through. Call on God. He wants to save, heal and deliver you. Call on God. He wants to use you. Call on God. He loves you. Call on God!

CHAPTER 2

TRUST IN GOD

EXPLORING THE EMOTION OF GUILT

But the Lord sent out a great wind into the sea, and there was a mighty tempest in the sea, so that the ship was like to be broken. 5) Then the mariners were afraid, and cried every man unto his god, and cast forth the wares that were in the ship into the sea, to lighten it of them. But Jonah was gone down into the sides of the ship; and he lay, and was fast asleep. 6) So the shipmaster came to him, and said unto him, What meanest thou, O sleeper? Arise, call upon thy God, if so be that God will think upon us, that we perish not. 7) And they said every one to his fellow, Come, and let us cast lots, that we may know for whose cause this evil is upon us. So they cast lots, and the lot fell upon Jonah. 8) Then said they unto him, Tell us, we pray thee, for whose cause this evil has come upon us; What is thine occupation? And whence comest thou? What is thy country? And of what people art thou? 9) And he said unto them, I am a Hebrew; and I fear the Lord, the God of heaven, which hath made the sea and the dry land.   *Jonah 1:4-9*

As we have seen in Chapter 1 verse 6, calling on God is not reserved exclusively for the pious. At one time or another, no matter who you are and no matter how big and bad you think you might be, when facing real trouble, you likely call on God. For example, when you think you are about to crash your car and slam helplessly on your breaks, you probably yell out, "Oh my God!" or "Jesus!" Well, this is exactly the point that the mariners aboard the cargo ship on which Jonah was traveling had reached.

The storm was mighty and so violent that these hardened, experienced sailors feared for their ship and for their very lives. They threw away their cargo since the money they had planned to make selling their goods in Tarshish would have proven useless had they drowned at sea. Seeing as that didn't work, they then called on their familiar gods but, of course, that failed. So, when the captain found Jonah asleep at the bottom of the ship, he woke him up and urged him to call on his God.

WHILE YOU WERE SLEEPING

How odd, though? With all of the chaos, panic, and struggle occurring around Jonah, he was sound asleep in the bottom of the ship. The captain, while desperately searching for someone or something to use to help save his ship, just happened to find him calmly asleep like nothing at all was going on. So, he said to Jonah (in so many words), "Wake up! The ship is tossing and turning, the sailors are running around and shouting, and the wind and the waves are raging. So how in the world can you sleep?" He probably thought to himself, "What is wrong with this man? Is he passed out drunk or something?"

The captain knew from experience that it was not normal for a person to sleep at a time like that. Most often, passengers on a ship caught in such a severe and terrible storm would be up and about trying to help. They would be trying to find out what was going on and asking would everything be all right or should they prepare to abandon ship. He knew that they would be doing something but certainly not sleeping.

So how could Jonah sleep through all of that confusion? I believe that Jonah felt guilty and depressed because he had disobeyed God. Jonah was asleep because he did not care what might have happened to him. He felt like a guilty man on death row and thought he deserved whatever came to him.

Jonah was like a little kid alone in his room at night hearing a noise or having a nightmare and then covering his head, pretending to be asleep so that the boogeyman won't see him. He knew that God had sent the storm after him and figured that, by ignoring it and sleeping through it, he would not be discovered.

And sometimes we do the same thing: We ignore and disobey God and then act like we're sleeping. Somehow, despite the storms, struggles, and chaos in our lives, we convince ourselves that God does not see us, that He's not paying attention. Worse, we convince ourselves that the storms, struggles, and chaos in our lives are okay or even normal and that sleeping through our troubles is a lot easier than getting things right with God.

In truth, though, it is better to get things right with God than to try to ignore God. As the prophet Ezekiel put it, there is no secret that you can hide from God. There is no thought or act that you can commit that God will not know about. God knows and sees all that you have done and will do. God knows and sees all that you are going through. In fact, it is quite possible that God sent the storm in your life to help you. You may think that the storm in your life is a mystery, but it is not. It is the Lord saying, "Return to me. I am the way, the truth, and the life. Return to me and I will make it all right."

IT'S NOT ME; IT'S YOU

We must remember that the weather appeared tempestuous for this particular ship only. For all the other ships at sea, all was calm. So due to this odd behavior of the storm and its severity, the sailors knew that there must have been some sort of divine intervention at work.

Now, we know that these sailors were no angels or choir boys. I am certain that all of these sailors had behaved badly at one time or another. Having been out at sea for weeks or even months at a time, whenever the sailors would come ashore, I'm certain that they would need to let off steam. The sailors would run around, chase women, drink, and fight.

However, I do not believe that any one sailor thought that it was him whom God was after at that particular moment. Whatever bad things the sailors did this time, while docked at Joppa, they probably had done a thousand times before. So, why would their gods or God be so angry now? I imagine the sailors figured that one of their shipmates had probably gone too far this time.

The sailors assumed that one of them had committed some sacrilege, cursed the gods, spit on someone's grave, murdered a baby, or raped a grandma. The sailors presumed that one of them had done something really outrageous to make the gods mad enough to send a storm after them. I say this because none of the sailors asked his god, "Is it me? Am I the guilty one?" I believe each of the sailors thought it was one of his shipmates who, was responsible for the storm because no one was talking or confessing that he had done wrong.

Parents, you experience this. You can be in one room watching television, using the computer, talking, cooking, cleaning, or doing whatever, and the kids can be in another room. Then suddenly, you hear a loud crash or bang. A vase, lamp, glass, or picture just broke. So, you get up, go into the room, and ask the kids, "What happened? Who broke what?" And, of course, nobody knows anything. Nobody saw anything. Nobody heard anything. Nobody did anything. The glass or picture just fell down and broke on its own.

So, you ask either the one whom you think did it or the one whom you think will tell who did it, "What happened?" If neither confesses nor tells on the other one, you then ask more questions.

"Were you standing next to it?" "No-o-o," they reply hesitantly. "Were you playing with it?" "No-o-o," they timidly say. "Are you sure?" "Ye-e-e-s-s," they shyly respond. Then, as your inquisition continues, they both get angry and say something like, "You always blame me. You never blame him," or "You never believe me. You always believe her." Now they both are upset and crying. Still, nobody knows anything, nobody saw anything, and nobody has confessed to anything. Then, you get upset and punish them both: "Go to your rooms and no television, no phone, and no computer!"

Well, the sailors felt that the gods were doing the same thing – punishing all of them for one person's wrong doing. However, none of the sailors wanted to die for someone else's crime. The sailors may have been willing to accept punishment for someone else had the penalty been a light one, like paying a fine or being beaten. But no sailor was prepared to die for his shipmate's offense.

As we read in Chapter 1 verse 7, *And they said every one to his fellow, Come, let us cast lots, that we may know for whose cause this evil has come upon us*. The sailors were essentially saying, "Let the gods (or fate) decide who is to blame."

To explain briefly, casting lots is when one person takes a handful of straws of equal length and then breaks one of the straws to make it shorter. He then places the straws in his hand making sure no one can tell how long they are. Finally, everyone draws a straw, and the person who picks the short straw is "it" or the one for whom they are looking.

OKAY, OKAY ... I CONFESS

So, they cast lots and the lot fell on Jonah. Jonah picked the short straw. Jonah most likely had hoped someone else would have picked the short straw. You see, Jonah had thought casting lots was just a matter of chance and that he probably would have been able to escape detection. However, he did not. The truth is Jonah could have saved the sailors the trouble of casting lots if he would have told them it was him whom the storm was sent to punish. Sadly, like most people and certainly most criminals, Jonah was not about to confess until he had absolutely no choice in the matter.

In fact, this reminds me of something that happened one Saturday when my son Drew was little and my daughter Starr was a baby. It was my wife Stephanie's birthday, so we decided to go to Atlantic City, a seaside resort in New

Jersey about two hours away from where we lived at the time. We asked Stephanie's mother to babysit and, since Stephanie had to direct and sing in the choir that Sunday morning, we planned to return that night to pick up the children. So, we got to Atlantic City and had a great time. Well, as we were walking along the boardwalk, getting ready to leave Atlantic City and head home, I saw from a distance, what looked like, my married cousin hugging and kissing on his wife.

So, I said to Stephanie, "There go my cousin and his wife. It is so nice that they are still in love." Then, Stephanie looked for a moment and said, "That may be your cousin, but that is *not* his wife." I said, "Yes it is. Who else would my married cousin be hugging and kissing on?" Stephanie looked again, only longer this time. I mean, she really studied them. Then Stephanie said, "That is *definitely not* his wife."

Unfortunately, I then became indignant, "Don't you think I know my own cousin and his wife? He's my cousin not yours. That is *my cousin,* and that is *his wife*!" But, Stephanie held fast and said, "*No-o-o.* She is *not.*" Well, this exchange soon turned into, let's say, a "heated discussion" about whether the woman was or was not my cousin's wife.

So, we finally decided that the only way to settle it was to speed up and see who she was. So we did, and when we got a close distance it became clear that Stephanie was right: That *was* my married cousin, but the woman he was hugging and kissing on was *definitely not* his wife.

So, this lead to another spirited exchange: "Now, what should we do? Should we turn around and go the other way?"
"No. That will take too long, and we have to get back to pick up the kids."
"Should we cross the street and act like we don't see them?"
"No. That will be too hard to do. He's my cousin, and he'll know it's me just like I knew it was him."
"Should we walk by and not speak?"
"No, that is crazy. Let's just go and say, 'Hello.' But we will not stay. We will tell him the truth: that we have to get back home to pick up the kids and that you have to sing and direct the choir in the morning."

So, we spoke. I said, "Hey, Cousin, what's up?" My cousin looked at me like he was seeing a ghost. He turned colors. He jumped back away from the woman. And he dropped her hand like it was hot! After a few seconds he replied, "H-h-hey, Cuz, w-what's up?" He then introduced the woman to us as his "co-worker". He stumbled over her name. I never actually caught it. Then he mumbled something like, "Since we're all in Atlantic City, we should hang out." We told him we would love to hang out with them, but we had to get back home to pick up the kids and Stephanie had to sing and direct the choir in the morning. And then we left.

Well, Sunday morning came, and Stephanie sang and directed the choir and it was great. The anointing fell, the pastor started preaching, and everyone was responding to the sermon. Then, right in the middle of the pastor's sermon, the same cousin whom we had seen in Atlantic City stood up and made *his own altar call*!

He walked down the aisle and stooped right in front of the pastor. The pastor stopped preaching, looked at my cousin, and started talking with him. Suddenly, the church went silent. The pastor prayed with my cousin and then asked my cousin's wife and child to come to the altar so he could pray with the three of them.

My cousin then announced to his wife, but loud enough for all to hear, "Baby, I am back! I am so-o-o sorry! I do not know what got into me. I must have been crazy. I must have lost my mind! But I am back! Please, forgive me. I want to save our marriage. I want to save our family. Baby, please forgive me. I am so, so sorry."

The pastor told my cousin's wife, "God has forgiven him and you should, too." My cousin was crying. His wife was crying. Their child was crying. Half of the people in the congregation were crying. Everyone could feel the suspense and tension in the air. This was real. This was powerful. This was emotional. What would my cousin's wife do?

After what seemed like an eternity, my cousin's wife said, "Ok, yes, yes …I will forgive him. I will take him back." The church erupted with shouts of joy and praise: "Oh, Hallelujah! Oh, thank you Jesus! Another marriage was saved from the brink of a break up! Satan is defeated! We have the victory! God has saved this family! Isn't it amazing? Isn't it wonderful? Oh, Hallelujah! Oh, thank you Jesus!"

Meanwhile, Stephanie and I were sitting in our seats unimpressed. We asked each other, "What do you think?"
"I do not know. What do you think?"
"Is this real?"
"No way..."
"Is he serious?"
"Maybe… but I really don't think so."

Then, my mother, who saw that we were debating instead of celebrating my cousin's reunion with his family, asked, "What is it with you two? Aren't you happy for your cousin? He has been forgiven. He has saved his marriage and family. Love and forgiveness have triumphed over selfishness and sin. Another marriage has been rescued from the brink of destruction. Satan is defeated, and we have the victory! Isn't it wonderful? Isn't it amazing?"

I said, "Mom, don't believe the hype. The only reason my cousin is here today doing all of this is because we saw him last night in Atlantic City hugging and kissing on another woman! We walked up to him while he was with her, so he knew he was cold busted. He must have thought we were going to tell his wife. Yea, he came here and did all of this, but I would not trust it. I do not think he is sincere at all. I think he just got caught and feels he had no choice but to confess."

Sure enough, not even two full weeks had passed by before my cousin moved out of the house and was back with the other woman. Like Jonah, my cousin did not sincerely confess. He had no real change of heart. He just had gotten caught. If the lot that the sailors had cast had not fallen on

Jonah, he would have said nothing. Likewise, if we had not seen my cousin in Atlantic City, *he* would have said nothing.

IT'S ALL ABOUT TRUST

The sad thing is that my cousin's wife trusted him. She obviously trusted him enough to marry him. He stood in the church and pledged both to God and her in front of all of his family and friends to love and cherish her and to forsake all others. And she believed him. But, what did he do? He broke the marriage vows and had an affair.

Of course, I do not know how good my cousin's relationship with his wife was at home, but even if they had a terrible one, he owed her the respect to try to work out their differences. And then, if they still could not get it together, he should have made an open, honest and clean break. On the contrary, he had the nerve to cheat, get caught, and make a dramatic public plea for his wife's forgiveness, only to turn around and break her trust two short weeks later. Can you believe it?

Sadly ... I do. Experience often teaches that if someone breaks your trust once, they will very likely do it again. Look, if your car broke down and left you stranded on the highway, you certainly would not trust driving it again until you took it to the mechanic to get it fixed. And even after getting the car repaired, it still might take a while before you trusted the car enough to take you anywhere and everywhere you need to go. And sometimes, you never truly feel comfortable with that car again.

Trusting people is a lot like trusting that car, and trust can be broken in so many ways. A woman meets a man; she likes him and he likes her. The woman asks, "Are you married or dating anyone?" The man says, "No, I am single." A few weeks or months after they have had sex and she has fallen in love, the truth comes out. The man is married, has a live-in girlfriend, or has two "baby's mommas".

On the other hand, trust in a mate can be broken before ever reaching the point of having a sexual affair. Often, a married person can become close with a co-worker or friend though the two have not yet had intimate contact. Perhaps, they have only flirted in person or via text, email, or phone; still it is an affair – an affair of the heart.

Such an "affair" can sometimes feel more real and intense than the person's marital relationship. The two share secrets, inside jokes, and cute expressions that only they find funny. And though it is not yet a sexual affair, in some ways, it is worse because the intimacy is so intense that it will eventually pull the married person towards extra-marital sex and out of his or her home.

Trust can also be broken by the mate who, while remaining sexually "faithful" to his or her spouse, chooses to retreat from marital troubles, life's disappointments, etc. by turning to some form of addiction. Perhaps, the person finds it is easier to self-medicate or withdraw completely from the marriage than it is to stand and fight for it. Therefore, he or she turns to alcohol, drugs, gambling, Pornography, domestic violence, flirting, or unbearable behavior, all of which are examples of broken trust as well. In a very real sense, addictions are forms of adultery because they act like mistresses: They take one's time, money and attention away from one's spouse.

Unfortunately, the one who takes a mistress (or mister) often shifts the blame to the spouse, saying, "It was your lack of love, respect, attention, or affection that forced me to seek comfort somewhere else." Or worse, he or she will often try to minimize the wrongdoing with words like, "What is the big deal? Everybody does it. It is just a little harmless fling;" or, "I only had a few beers [a few joints, etc.]." Or the guilty party will say something like, "Honey I know that we set a budget, but I really needed this dress [shirt, shoes, golf club, sofa, etc.]."

Furthermore, trust can be breached by a parent toward a kid. And let's not think for a moment that trust is a trivial issue for a child. On the contrary, it is extremely significant. So, it is not okay to tell your kids that you're going to buy them something or take them somewhere or spend time with them and say, "… something else came up" and not do it. No matter how valid your reason may be for disappointing them, it is still a breach of their trust. And let's face it; you are your kid's primary example – whether good or bad – of keeping one's word and earning one's trust.

And trust is hard to get back, once it has been broken, because the truth is we barely trust ourselves. Statistics show 80% of all New Year's Eve resolutions are broken within the first two months. Therefore, if we cannot keep our word to ourselves and if we cannot trust ourselves, how well can we trust others? That is why Jesus Christ's second great commandment is *…love [your] neighbor as [yourself]* (Mark 12:31). We must have a reference point for love and trust. If we can love ourselves, then we can love others; and, if we can trust ourselves, then the possibility exists that we can trust others.

THE GREATEST LOVE OF ALL

So then, the question arises: How do we develop love and trust toward others, as well as toward ourselves? The answer, simply stated, is we can learn to love and trust ourselves when we come to understand the love that God first had toward us. You see, while we were yet in sin, untrustworthy, lying, cheating, doing our own thing, and not thinking about God, Christ died for us.

In fact, some of us seemed almost unlovable based on the way we had been treated and mistreated. Some of us felt so rejected and unwanted, even by the people that should have loved us, that we thought we would always be alone and unaccepted. Yet, like the stone which the builders rejected, God saw the value in you and me. Like the Jewish orphan girl, Esther, whom Mordecai reared to become queen, God knows what you are destined to be. Like the short, smelly shepherd boy, David, whose family considered him an odd little poet, God saw him as an anointed king. Remember, man looks at the outward appearance, but God looks at the heart.

No matter what has been done to you and no matter what you have gone through, God does love you. God cares and He sees all the potential. He sees all that you can and will do. And because He loves you and me so much, He does not want us to be lost. That is why He gave His only begotten son, Jesus Christ, to pay the price on the cross for our sins.

All we have to do is accept it. Accept that God loves us and sees value in us. Accept that Jesus thought we were worth dying for, worth rising for, and worth living for. Then, as we begin to see ourselves as God sees us, we can begin to love ourselves based on the love that He has for us.

Fortunately, God's love is not fleeting. The love of God is not based on how we make Him feel or if we do everything exactly right, which is a good thing because I know I would be left out in the cold. I would be trying to avoid my guilt and shame like Jonah, hiding at the bottom of the boat.

Rather, God's love is steadfast, unmovable, and always abounding. He said ... *I will never leave [you], nor forsake [you]* (Hebrews 13:5). That means no matter what you have gone through, He will *never* turn his back on you. Jesus is the same yesterday, today and forever. You can always trust and depend on God. And when we learn to trust God's love toward us and begin to love and trust Him in return, we then can begin to love and trust ourselves and, by extension, begin to open up to loving and trusting others.

I understand that love and trust are not established overnight. Even learning to love and trust ourselves takes time. Start small by setting simple goals that are easy to attain. For example, if you want to lose weight, do not tell yourself, "I am going to the gym six days per week at 4:00 in the morning, and I'm going to work out for five hours each day. In addition, I will run ten miles per day and eat only lunch." These are unrealistic beginner goals that will set you up for failure and set you back into self-mistrust.

No, it is better to set sensible goals that are possible to achieve but still require some real effort. For example, start walking three times per week for thirty minutes each time, and then work your way up. Each month, increase your level and time of exercise and, before you know it, you will be walking longer, faster, and more frequently. And try eating smaller portions at meal time. Let's say, eat one chicken breast instead of two. You can do it!

In addition, you can establish trust with your family. Keep your word and, over time, your spouse and children will be certain that you will deliver on what you promise.

Of course, this means being sexually faithful, but it also means doing chores faithfully, staying within the agreed upon family budget, keeping promises regarding dropping off, picking up, and spending time with your kids, and paying bills and keeping appointments promptly. And your family, in turn, can establish trust with you.

Now, I admit we cannot put all of our trust in any human being. After all, none of us has yet attained Sainthood; rather, we are saints in the making. The 118th Psalm verse 8, (which happens to be the middle verse of the Bible) reminds us, *It is better to trust in the Lord than to put confidence in man.* Even our government knows this because on the dollar is printed, "In God we trust." So, in our quest to embrace trust for ourselves and for others, remember, above all, to trust in God. God will never leave you, lie to you, nor let you down.

Trust in God, Who made the land and sea. Trust in God, Who neither slumbers nor sleeps. Trust in God, Who cares for you and me. Trust in God concerning your marriage and family. Trust in God concerning your guilt. Trust in God concerning your addictions. Trust in God to be healthy. Trust in God to be prosperous. Trust in God to be victorious. Trust in God; He is the one and only sure foundation.

ALWAYS AND FOREVER TRUE

We can trust that what God says, He surely will do. God's word *must* accomplish what it says. God spoke a word and created heaven and earth, and it all would pass away before He would allow "one jot or one tittle" of His word to go unfulfilled. God's word hung the sun, moon, and stars in the sky, and they have not come down yet.

Furthermore, He said He would never again destroy the world by water and, despite hurricane Katrina in New Orleans and the tsunami in Japan, the world still exists. God's word simply cannot return to Him void of accomplishing what He sets it out to do.

That is precisely why God sent the storm after Jonah. God's word told Jonah to go and cry against Nineveh, and God trusted Jonah to obey His word. But sadly, Jonah broke God's trust and went the other way. How silly of Jonah? He forgot that God can use anything – the wind, the rain, a storm, a raven, even a donkey – to achieve whatever He wills.

Jonah was foolish to have thought he could escape God's presence. What mountain could Jonah have climbed to escape God's presence, when God uses the earth as His footstool? What valley could he have descended to escape God's presence, when David said, *If I make my bed in hell … [God is] there*? What sea could Jonah have crossed or what country could Jonah have hidden in to escape God's presence, when God spoke the seas and the land into existence?

No one can run or hide from God. God is everywhere, and He is the Creator of everything. The Scriptures decree, *The earth is the Lord's, and the fullness thereof; the world, and they that dwell therein* (Psalm 24:1). Even *the heavens declare the glory of God; and the firmament showeth his handiwork* (Psalm 19:1). Jonah had it twisted. Instead of trying to run *from* God's presence, Jonah should have been trying to get *into* God's presence. As the Psalmist David said, *I was glad when they said unto me, Let us go into the house of the Lord. Peace be within thy walls, and prosperity within thy palaces* (Psalm 122:1, 7).

In God's presence is the fullness of joy. In God's presence are healing, deliverance and victory. In God's presence is where we should want to be.

However, Jonah wanted to flee from the presence of God. He acted like a spoiled little kid who runs away from home because he doesn't want to do what Daddy and Mommy tells him to do. In fact, I remember running away from home at the age of eight. I stuffed my lunch box with candy and a peanut butter and jelly sandwich. I took my dog and my clarinet, and I was leaving. But, I don't think I made it four blocks before I had to use the bath room. Believe it or not, running away from home is not that easy at eight years of age. There are details involved in running away that, in the heat of the moment, get overlooked, like where to go to the bathroom and where to sleep. So, I ended up going to my friend's house, and his mother let me in to use their bathroom. She was nice to me: She gave me some ice cream and called my parents. Of course, my parents were relieved and came to pick me up. And although they forgave me for running away, they still made me do whatever it was they had told me to do in the first place.

I think God did the same thing with Jonah as my parents did with me. As the loving Parent that God is, He allowed Jonah to attempt to run away.

I can see God saying to Himself, "How cute? Jonah had his little adventure. He got to go on a boat ride and take a nap. But now, it is time for Jonah to get back to work and do what I told him to do in the first place." See, Jonah still had a job to do. If God's word says you are going to do something, you can try to escape, you can attempt to ignore it, or you can aim to drown out His voice with partying, drugs, or whatever foolishness you choose. But, when it is all said and done, God's will shall, be done because His word is always and forever true.

I'M A CHRISTIAN, AND I TRUST IN GOD

That is why it is impossible to run away from God, because His ever-abiding word will find you wherever you run or wherever you think you might hide. And when you belong to Him, once you have given your life to Christ, no matter how much you attempt to blend in with the crowd, you will stick out like a sore thumb. Something about you, however indescribable, will say to those around you, "He doesn't belong here. Who is he?" or "Where does she come from? What is she doing here?" Somehow, something will alert them to the fact that you are peculiar and out of place.

47

So it was with Jonah. That is why the sailors, having observed Jonah's odd behavior of sleeping in the midst of all the mayhem aboard the tossing cargo ship, decided to cast lots. When the lot fell on Jonah, it then became obvious to them that he was more than just any old stranger catching a ride on their ship. And thus began the questions: "What do you do? Where do you come from? What nationality are you?" Jonah replied *... I am a Hebrew; and I fear the Lord, the God of heaven, which hath made the sea and the dry land* (Jonah 1:9). In essence, Jonah was announcing his guilt for having offended the God of the Hebrews – the only One powerful enough to send the wind and storm after him.   At the same time, Jonah was testifying or witnessing to the sailors. Jonah was letting the sailors know they no longer needed to worship or serve any other gods, because there was but one true and living God, the God he served. And by saying, "I am a Hebrew," Jonah was identifying himself by his religion, much like if you or I today were to say, "I am a Christian or follower of Christ."

In addition, Jonah said, "I fear the Lord." The phrase "fear the Lord" in the Old Testament referred to reverence or trust. Thus, Jonah was saying, "I trust in the Lord," which goes to show that Jonah was a lot like us. Many of us *say* we are Christians and we trust in God. We go to church and hear the preacher speak God's word. Some of us read and study the scriptures and even use pink, green, or yellow highlighters. But, then, we go out and do just the opposite of what God's word tells us to do. God's word says that we should "have no other gods before Him". Yet, many of us serve money and worship at the feet of our televisions, computers, smart phones, and iPads. God's word tells us to "love one another" and to "love our enemies". Yet, we often respond to others with irritation and petty jealousy. These are all examples of claiming to follow and trust God yet running the other way.

In fact, claiming to know and trust God but turning away from Him just may be worse than being an all-out sinner. Why? A sinner who has not yet received the word of God is like the sailors being tossed in the midst of the storm of life but do not know why. We, however, who claim to be Christians, claim to trust God, and claim to have received God's word but still run away, are like Jonah – disobedient children treading upon God's grace and mercy. ***For unto whomsoever much is given, of him shall be much required...*** (Luke 12:48).

I believe this is the reason that so many of us Christians often have strong winds and storms raging in our lives. We are trying to go our own way instead of obeying and trusting in God's word. But, if we would just wake up from our sleep, wake up from our depression, and wake up from our delusions and say, "I am a Christian, and I trust in God," this statement would begin to reaffirm our faith as followers of Jesus Christ.

Know that God does not give you instructions to embarrass you, nor does He give you His word to torture or hurt you. God gives you His word because He wants the best for you. So, whatever the test or task might be, however challenging it might seem, encourage yourself with, "I am a Christian, and I trust in God." When the winds of guilt, anger, depression, and delusion are tossing and churning the sea of your life, trust in God. Things will not always be this way; they will get better.

Oh, I know that the storm in your life can get so bad that you may have to lose some cargo or let some things, maybe even certain family and friends, go. And, yes, it can be really hard to let them go. Making a change in your life can feel like you are rowing against the wind. Progress can seem so slow. Still, trust in God.

Even if it seems you will never be free from pain, struggles, addictions, or strongholds, do not believe the enemy. Jesus died on the cross for you and me. Satan thought he had won. Satan thought he had the victory. But, after three days, Jesus rose from the grave and declared ... *All power is given unto me in heaven and in earth* (Matthew 28:18). Jesus defeated sin, death and the grave so that you and I might be free.

Trust in God, and you will have the victory. Trust in God because you are a Christian, and it is time that you start living and believing like one. And if you are not a Christian, then become one right now by confessing with your mouth that "Jesus is Lord" and believing in your heart that God rose him from the dead (Romans 10:9).

Then, find a word-based church where you can grow and mature as a follower of Christ. No matter what is going on in your life, encourage yourself. As long as there is breath in your body, all is not lost; there is still hope. Make this affirmation: "I am a Christian, and I trust in the true and living God." Confess it until you believe and receive it: "I am a Christian, and I trust in God!" Trust in God.

CHAPTER 3

GOD HAS PREPARED A PLACE FOR YOU

A CLOSER LOOK AT THE EMOTION OF GUILT

Then were the men exceedingly afraid, and said unto him," Why hast thou done this?" … The men knew that he fled from the presence of the Lord, because he had told them. 11) Then said they unto him," What shall we do unto thee, that the sea may be calm unto us?" For the sea wrought and was tempestuous. 12) And he said unto them, Take me up, and cast me forth into the sea; so shall the sea be calm unto you: for I know that for my sake this great tempest is upon you. 13) Nevertheless the men rowed hard to bring it to the land; but they could not: for the sea wrought, and was tempestuous against them. 14) Wherefore they cried unto the Lord, and said, We beseech thee, O Lord, we beseech thee, let us not perish for this man's life, and lay not upon us innocent blood: for thou, O Lord, hast done as it pleased thee. 15) So they took up Jonah, and cast him forth into the sea: and the sea ceased from her raging.

16) Then the men feared the Lord exceedingly, and offered a sacrifice unto the Lord, and made vows. 17) Now the Lord had prepared a great fish to swallow up Jonah. And Jonah was in the belly of the fish three days and three nights.
Jonah 1:10-17

In this portion of our text, the sailors were exceedingly afraid for their lives because of the tempest that God had sent toward their ship after Jonah. As we previously discovered in Chapter 1 verse 9, Jonah admitted to his responsibility for the sailors' turmoil by confessing that he was a Hebrew and that his God – the One from Whom, he was fleeing – was the One Who made the sea and land. Thus, the sailors began to question Jonah: "Why have you done this to us?! Why have you involved us in *your* mess? Are you nuts?!" You are behaving so selfishly and irresponsibly by placing us between yourself and a God you say is powerful enough to send a terrible storm after you. You just told us you serve the God of heaven, Who made the sea and dry land. So, what on earth made you think you could have run away? Now, your God is angry with us because of your foolishness, because of something that you did!!"

IN BAD COMPANY

It had become clear to the sailors that Jonah's selfish actions were the cause of all their trouble. And I know just how those sailors felt because, when I was a little kid, I had a cousin (*not* the one mentioned in **Chapter 2: Trust in God**) who was always getting me into trouble. I remember, once, when I was at his house, he said, "Come on, Dennis. I left my bicycle over my friend's house, and I want to get it back." I said, "Okay."

So, we went to a house and rang the doorbell, but nobody answered the door. Next, my cousin went into the backyard, took the bike, and said he would call his friend later to tell him he had taken his bicycle back. So, we left. Well, as we were walking down the street with the bicycle, after having passed about two or three houses, three boys came running after us. One of them was yelling, "Hey, that guy is stealing my bicycle!" Apparently, my knucklehead cousin just had walked into somebody's backyard and *stolen* a bicycle.

Anyway, my cousin hopped onto the bicycle to get away while I had to run. Fortunately, I was a fast runner back then and was able to get away, which was a good thing for me. Had those boys caught up with me, I'm sure they would have beaten me up for something my crazy cousin had done. And all I was guilty of was being at the wrong place at the wrong time with the wrong person. My cousin knew, when we left his house, that he was planning to steal a bicycle, but I had no idea.

Experiences such as the one I faced make one wonder why people, like my cousin and Jonah, fail to consider how their actions might affect other people. Maybe they are just so self-absorbed, believing the world revolves around them, that they think anything they do – good or bad – is okay, as long as it benefits them. You see, a narcissist (or self-centered person) will tell lies, cheat, steal, gamble, take drugs, commit fraud, and ignore and mistreat family and friends. But, how their actions might affect anyone else is secondary to their own needs being met.

Look, I would be dishonest if I were to say that, while growing up, I never did anything wrong. But, I got saved at an early age and was about fourteen when I received the Holy Ghost, so I never was much of a tough guy. And what meager mischief I did, I would always get caught doing. Somehow, people who knew me or my parents would always see or find out about whatever wrong I had done and would immediately tell my parents. Amazingly, it was the unsaved people, the "un-churched" ones, who would seem the most disappointed by my misbehavior. They would ask, "What is going on, Dennis? What is wrong? Why did you do that? I thought you were saved. I thought you were a Christian." I would feel like Jonah being interrogated by the sailors, "Why have you done this? Why would you try to escape God's presence? You should know better."

REGRET – A HARD PILL TO SWALLOW

This is why you should not try to hide or run away from God. Once Christ has entered your life, you are not the same. You are no longer your own. You become a child of the King of kings, a child of the God of all heaven and earth. There is simply no escaping God's presence. Even if you decide to go back to your old crowd and restart your old habits, it will not be the same. For some reason, it will not feel right. You will feel like you just do not fit in any more.

And if you say, "I will go somewhere else where no one will know me, and I will do my own thing in a crowd where no one will pay attention to me," it will not work. You still will stand out.

Moreover, your conscience will not let you escape. You will begin to ask yourself questions, like, "Why did I do that? What is wrong with me? I know better. I was raised better than that." Your sense of right and wrong will feel upset or violated. Your conscience will speak to you like it spoke to Jonah in verse 10 of the text through the voice of the sailors, who said to him...*Why hast thou done this? For the men knew that he fled from the presence of the Lord, because he had told them.* You will begin to question yourself as I imagine Jonah did: "Why didn't I just do what the Lord told me to do and go cry against Nineveh? What is wrong with me? I know better than to disobey the Lord." You see, guilt – that emotion or feeling we struggle with when questioning our actions – eventually causes us to feel responsible for what we have done wrong (or, like in Jonah's case, what we have failed to do right.) And it is this emotion of guilt which leads us to subsequent feelings of shame, regret, and self-doubt.

I know whereof I speak regarding the emotion of guilt and its haunting effects. In my adult past, I have done so many messed up things that I can hardly express the magnitude of guilt I used to carry. However, I will share one example out of many. After dating a girl for two years, I asked her to marry me. We grew up in the same church, so my family knew her family and everybody got along fine. We have all seen those young couples that seemed so right for each other that it appeared as though they were destined to be together. Well, that was us.

Anyway, during my sophomore year of dental school, I gave her an engagement ring and we set a wedding date. She was thrilled as she planned our wedding. She picked out her bridal gown and sent out all the invitations. Her family even placed an announcement of our coming nuptials in the newspaper.

Well, one day, I happened to be thumbing through the newspaper. I was looking for the sports page or the funnies, not even recalling that the announcement was to appear in that particular day's news, when suddenly I saw it: *Mr. and Mrs. So-and- So are pleased to announce the engagement and forthcoming marriage of their daughter, So-and-so, to Dr. Dennis W. Jackson, etc.*

I saw the picture and the announcement, and I do not know what happened to me but I panicked. I was into planning the wedding and the idea of getting married up until that precise moment. But, once I saw it in *print,* I bugged out and backed out of the wedding. Just like a scene in a movie, I left without any explanation or a single word. I went back to dental school and hid. And when I say that I hid, I mean I did not come back home from school for two years. I left her having to answer all the questions, and she really did not know what happened because I really did not know what happened.

Now, I know that everyone is different, and each of us has his or her own unique story. However, truthfully speaking, we all have done something for which we have felt guilt. It could have been something as simple as talking too much or divulging too much.

Admittedly, I am often at fault in this area. I don't do it on purpose but, unless I really focus, I find myself running my big mouth and saying too much. So, do not tell me any secrets or juicy gossip because, if I start talking to someone else, I am certain to slip up and let it out. Then, I spend the next three days beating myself up for being a blabber mouth.

In actuality, many people carry the burden of guilt. Teenagers, for example, may experience guilt for lying to their parents about their activities, such as taking drugs, having sex, or cutting school. Believe it or not, most people, even teenagers, want to be honest. Some men feel guilt for having fathered children whom they never raised or nurtured. Some women bear guilt for having aborted their unborn babies. Years later, they still know what they did was wrong and miss the children they could have cared for and loved. Certain men or women carry guilty feelings for having abandoned a spouse. Perhaps, they married too young or too hastily, and they suddenly left, choosing not to deal with the marriage anymore.

Moreover, there are those who suffer guilt for various other reasons. Some feel at fault for being workaholics, overachievers, or too competitive. Others blame themselves for being slackers, underachievers, or unsuccessful. Some feel blameworthy for giving in too easily and being yes-men.

Still, others feel culpable for being too stern and always saying, "No". The truth is almost any behavior, thought, feeling, or action can cause one to feel compunction. And everyone has done something for which they feel some level of remorse because all have sinned and fallen short of God's glory (Romans 3:23).

So, we see that Jonah felt guilty. As he and the sailors experienced the tumultuous storm, Jonah knew he was to blame. Jonah knew that he was the target of God's wrath. He knew he was the reason for the tempest; he knew he was the reason for the sailors' lives being at risk; and, he knew he was the reason for their cargo – the sailors' source of income – being tossed overboard.

A CRY FOR HELP

Then said they unto him, What shall we do unto thee, that the sea may be calm unto us (Jonah 1: 11)? Jonah obviously was to blame for the sailors' misfortune; yet, they showed him kindness by asking, "How can we help? What can we do for *you*? How can we help *you* appease your God so that the sea will calm down?"

Know that whenever you are being deluged by emotions of guilt and shame, the people around you will notice. They will see that you are in a typhoon of troubles and, like the sailors, will offer to help you. They may even refer you to a counselor or psychologist.

Here's a friendly tip: If people you know (like your family or friends) are telling you to seek professional help, then you are probably showing signs that the ship of your life is on a stormy sea. Though to you it may be unrecognizable, to those around you it will be evident that the ship of your life has veered into turbulent waters.

However, you must know that seeing a counselor or psychotherapist will not be enough to steer you back into steady seas. Yes, it may help you to talk about your past – about what your parents did or did not do for you; about what adolescent adversities affected you; or, about how your siblings, peers, teachers, family, or friends unfavorably influenced you. But, you must be careful not to fall into faulting everyone else for the tempestuous times that befall you.

Frankly, most of the guilt we carry is due to choices we did or did not make or how we reacted to various events in our lives. So, instead of seeking out someone else to blame, we should, like Jonah, ultimately take responsibility for the consequences we find ourselves facing.

Above all, we should call on Jesus, who can speak to the winds and the waves of our minds and say, "Peace, be still," knowing that they must obey him. Turning to Jesus is our only answer and key for living guilt-free lives.

Take note that, although Jonah had been discovered, by his own admission, to be the one whom the storm had been sent after, the tempest still had not ceased. So, the sailors asked Jonah, "How can we help you appease your God?" They figured he, as the prophet of God which he (in verse 10) told them he was, would know better than anyone how to placate his angry God.

Interestingly, the sailors never appeared to be harsh with, cruel toward, or judgmental of Jonah. And one could argue that the sailors had every right to be livid with him for putting their lives and money in jeopardy.

One could learn a lot from the sailors about how to treat somebody who is in trouble. If you see someone racked with guilt and shame, be patient and kind toward them. Pray for them. Remember, *all* have sinned and fallen short of the glory of God. *All* of us make mistakes at some time or another. We are all just fortunate enough that God often does not publicly expose us.

TOUGH LOVE

Evidently, the sailors' benevolence toward Jonah finally pierced his conscience because, in verse 12, he became repentant toward them. *And he said unto them, Take me up, and cast me forth into the sea; so shall the sea be calm unto you: for I know that for my sake this great tempest is upon you.* At last, Jonah took responsibility for all the trouble the sailors had been experiencing. He finally realized his actions had consequences that affected everyone else on the ship, and he did not want the sailors to suffer for his sake any longer.

On that note, if we do sin, we must not stay in sin. We must not continue in guilt, allowing those in the ship of life with us – our family, friends, and fellow Christians – to suffer for our wrongdoings. Like Jonah, we must be prepared to do whatever it takes to make things right with God, even if it costs our lives.

By telling the sailors to cast him into the sea, Jonah was essentially saying, "All of this is my fault, and only I can make things right." This was a true admission by Jonah because, when God sends a storm after someone, there is nothing you can do to rescue him or her.

Whether you are a parent, spouse, or concerned friend, you cannot help enough, you cannot give enough, you cannot sacrifice enough, and you cannot do enough to assuage the blustery seas of his or her circumstances. You can even throw your goods overboard, but it all will be lost. You can spend all of your time, money, attention, and resources in efforts to save the person, and it all will be for nothing. The sea will calm only when the one whom God sends the storm after deals with the Lord for him or herself.

Oddly, scholars say that Jonah is a type of Christ who was willing to give his life to save others. However, I tend to disagree. Jonah disobeyed God, and it was his disobedience and sin that precipitated the storm, which subsequently endangered his own life, as well as the lives of the sailors. Jesus, on the other hand, knew no sin; he was perfectly and completely blameless and upright. No punishment was being directed toward the Savior for any personal disobedience on his part.

Instead, Jesus died on the cross to pay the price for our universal disobedience. Then, in three days, he arose from the grave declaring victory over sin. Now, all one must do to be sin and guilt-free is repent and be baptized in the name of Jesus Christ, and he or she can live a life of victory.

Even though Jonah told the sailors to throw him into the sea, we see, in verses 13-14 of our text, the sailors were reluctant to do so. Perhaps, the sailors thought that Jonah appeared too remorseful or too eager to be thrown overboard. It is one thing to say, "Yea, my bad, I was wrong. Please, forgive me." After all, guilt and shame are normal emotions, which tell us we have limits. None of us is superman or superwoman. We all can and will make mistakes.

And, like it or not, at some point in our lives, we all need help. One could say that guilt and shame lead to humility and spirituality because they help us realize that we are not God, and we really do need His help, love, forgiveness, direction, and protection.

However, there are those who carry guilt and shame too far, to the point where they begin to attack and destroy their own self-image. They say negative things, like, "I am no good. I am bad, evil, and unworthy of God's love, forgiveness, and concern. Bad stuff always happens to me. Things never go my way. I am such a loser."

This kind of defeatist self-talk leads to self-hate and subsequent self-destructive behavior, such as, taking drugs, abusing alcohol, etc., in despondent efforts to self-inflict punishment or pain.

It is quite possible that Jonah thought that God would not forgive him; or, perhaps, Jonah could not forgive himself. Or maybe, just maybe, the sailors thought that Jonah was trying to kill himself.

Remember, previously, while everyone else on the ship was trying to fight and survive the terrible storm, Jonah had been found alone, sleeping at the bottom of the ship.

So, clearly, the sailors thought that Jonah already had been acting strangely, to say the least. Thus, the sailors made every attempt not to throw Jonah overboard. But, the harder they rowed, the harder the wind blew. As we read in verse 13 ... *the men rowed hard to bring it to the land; but they could not: for the sea wrought, and was tempestuous against them.*

All too often, the same occurs when family and friends try to help a loved one ensnared by sinful guilt, shame, or depression. Their well-intended efforts simply will not work. Instead, the person with the problem must first acknowledge that he (or she) needs help. He must acknowledge that God loves him, that God will forgive him, and that he needs God to step in. It is common knowledge that one cannot make an alcoholic or drug addict stop using and abusing if he does not want to stop.

Nor can one make a lying, cheating spouse stop being dishonest and unfaithful if he (or she) does not want to stop. Surely, one can reason with him, argue with him, or kick him out of the house. But, until he decides for himself that he will do whatever is necessary to stop his wrong behavior, he simply will continue in his error.

In truth, neither you nor I can manipulate or force anyone to do anything. Realizing this fact is what tough love is all about: You must love the person with the problem enough to let him (or her) be responsible for and suffer the consequences of his own actions. This does not mean that you have stopped caring for him.

On the contrary, it means that you love him enough to let him pursue the path he has chosen. And, sometimes, you really do have to cast him into the sea because as long as you are in the boat rowing as hard as you can for him, he will continue to sleep and ignore the problem. In fact, he may even complain it is your fault that he is not sailing smoothly through life. Like Jonah prior to his confession, he may gladly let you bear the burden of calming the stormy seas of his life.

He may let you pay *his* bills, make *his* excuses, and fix *his* problems. And, in the end, it will be *you, not him*, who will feel stressed out and guilty for what is not at all your responsibility.

GUILT IS A TWO-EDGED SWORD

I imagine that, as the sailors rowed harder, they made a little headway, but the wind just blew them back again. You know the saying, "one step forward but two steps backward." This is how it goes when you try to rescue someone from a storm, which God sent for that individual. As much as you may truly want to help, your efforts prove useless because you cannot stand against the wind of God's counsel and you cannot stop the tide of God's judgment.

Ironically, the thing that drives you to want to intervene on behalf of your loved one is the same thing that he or she is struggling with in the first place – the emotion of guilt.

When it is all said and done, you don't want to feel like a bad parent, unloving spouse, or unconcerned friend. You don't want to be left with regret, feeling like you didn't do everything you possibly could have done to help. You don't want to have to say, "I could have, would have, or should have done more or been there more."

That is precisely why the sailors did not quickly grab Jonah and toss him into the sea. They rowed harder because they did not want to have to live with feelings of guilt, shame, or regret.

However, what we often fail to realize is that our loved one, spouse, child, or friend is actually one of God's children. We forget that the person is in God's hands, and God, the loving Parent that He is, knows what He is doing. God sent the storm after Jonah not because He hated him. On the contrary, it was because of His immense love for Jonah that He did not want him to remain in the error of his ways.

So it is with that individual with whom God is dealing. Hebrews 12:6 reminds us that the Lord chastens those whom He loves. God sends the storm into the life of your loved one because He loves and wants to correct him. He said, *I will never leave thee, nor forsake thee* (Hebrews 13:5). God knows what he is going through, and He sends the storm because He wants him to grow beyond selfishness and sin to sharing and showing the steadfast and amazing love, which God has toward us all.

In truth, we remain responsible for our children up to a certain age, but once they have become of age and are out of the house, they must begin to take mature responsibility for their own actions. Moreover, we who are already adults must not continue to blame our parents for things that went wrong in our lives. At some point, we all must be held accountable for the choices we make. God created us as free-will agents and gave us freedom of choice. Therefore, we choose how we respond to events, to people, and, most importantly, to God. Selfishness, sin, guilt, and shame are traps that hold us in bondage to our past, but Jesus died on the cross and rose from the grave so that we might be free: free from blaming ourselves and others; free from unhappy memories; free to achieve life's beauty; and, free to enjoy peace, love, forgiveness, prosperity and victory.

Due to all that had transpired the sailors became convinced that Jonah's God was the only true God. Thus, the sailors finally gave up. They gave up summoning their false gods, they gave up rowing, they gave up fighting, and they began praying. Only this time, they prayed to the Lord God of Israel. The sailors earnestly prayed because it had become painfully obvious to them that they had no alternative to calm the angry sea than to hoist Jonah into it. Thus, they begged God not to punish them for honoring Jonah's request. They did not want innocent blood on their hands. After all, what if the lot that had fallen on Jonah was wrong?

71

But in actuality, they knew this was God's will at work. As verse 14 of our text reads…
Wherefore they cried unto the Lord, and said, We beseech thee, O Lord, we beseech thee, let us not perish for this man's life, and lay not upon us innocent blood: for thou, O Lord, hast done as it pleased thee. The sailors were saying, "Please do not punish us for doing exactly what "You" want us to do.

Similarly, those of us with loved ones caught up in the midst of a sinful storm, like lying, cheating, gambling, etc., will eventually find ourselves praying this prayer: "Lord, I have done all that I could to help So-and-so, but I just cannot do it any longer. I have reached the end of my rope. Father, I give him (or her) over to "You". He is in "Your hands."

And then you must "let go and let God" and not feel guilty about it because you did not cause the storm in your loved one's life in the first place. That storm is between God and That person. No matter how much your loved tone might blame you, do not blame yourself. Remember, as long as you keep him in the ship with you, the blustering wind will blow on you, and then you will *both* go down with the ship. So, just pray. Pray for him, pray for yourself, and then let the storm, which God sent for him, have its way with him. Don't worry; God loves you and him, and He knows what He is doing.

IT IS ALL PART OF THE PLAN

The sailors finally recognized that they had been just like the wind, the sea, and the lot. God had used them all to bring Jonah back to Himself. That is why we must realize that, when it comes to our loved ones, God is working everything out for His divine purpose. So, when we let our loved ones go off into the stormy sea, God will not hold it against us. In fact, God will be pleased. As we saw in verse 15, once the sailors threw Jonah overboard, *the sea ceased from her raging.* The storm finally ceased because it got what it had come for. And to top it off, the Lord was glorified. As verse 16 reads, *Then the men feared the Lord exceedingly, and offered a sacrifice unto the Lord, and made vows.* The Sovereign Lord knows how to work everything and everyone according to His divine plan.

Now the Lord had prepared a great fish to swallow up Jonah (Jonah 1:17). The Lord was prepared. He knew what He had planned. Although… I'm sure Jonah had his doubts. I mean, can you imagine how Jonah must have felt when the sailors grabbed him? He must have thought, "This is it. I am going to drown in the sea." I know that if I were him, I would have been in a full panic, begging, kicking, and screaming, "Somebody, help me! Save me. I didn't mean it! I change my mind; let's row some more!"

But, actually, being thrown overboard was exactly what Jonah needed because he had to die to his disobedience. We all must die to sin, selfishness, and disobedience. And sometimes, being thrown into the unknown is precisely what we need.

The Lord, in His sovereignty, knows what He has prepared for us. We cannot see the future. Once we have been tossed overboard, we cannot see what lies beneath the water waiting for us. Apostle Paul said we see through a glass but darkly (or dimly). Only God can see clearly what He has prepared for us. Only God knows what lies ahead for us.
But this one thing we do know – He loves and cares for us. And He will never leave nor forsake us, no matter what we have done and no matter what has been done to us. That is why the Lord prepared a great fish for Jonah. God prepared a place for him. He had already made a way for Jonah out of no way.

GOD HAS PREPARED A PLACE FOR YOU

Just when you think it is all over and you cannot see your way,
Remember, friend, the Lord has already prepared a way.
No habit, addiction, or stronghold can keep you
When God has prepared a way out for you.

You do not have to feel guilty.
The Lord has prepared a place for you to breathe.
Though the ship of your life has broken in two,
The Lord has prepared a place for it, too.

The Lord wants to comfort, bless, and keep you.
The Lord has prepared a place for you.
Cast your sins, guilt, and shame into the sea.
The Lord's love and forgiveness will comfort you and me.

No matter what others may say or do,
The Lord has prepared a hiding place for you.
Let go of the past; it will trap and hurt you.
The Lord has prepared a bright future for you.

You do not have to be racked with guilt and shame;
Just wholly lean on Jesus Christ's name.
Jesus already paid the price for you.
Jesus suffered on the cross for the wrong you may do.

No matter what you have done, the Lord loves you.
He has prepared a way of escape for you.
Do not give up. You are not alone.
God does not watch idly from His throne.

He sees all that you are going through.
And He is actively working things out for you.
God has prepared a place for you, a place to rest, pray

and breathe.
The Lord has prepared a place for you, and He has
prepared a place for me.

CHAPTER 4

GOD'S CURE FOR DEPRESSION

UNCOVERING DEPRESSION

And Moses answered and said, But, behold, they will not believe me, nor hearken unto my voice: for they will say, The Lord hath not appeared unto thee. 2) And the Lord said unto him," What is that in thine hand?" And he said," A rod". 3) And he said, Cast it on the ground. And he cast it on the ground, and it became a serpent; and Moses fled from before it. 4) And the Lord said unto Moses, Put forth thine hand, and take it by the tail. And he put forth his hand, and caught it, and it became a rod in his hand: *Exodus 3:1-4*
Then Jonah prayed unto the Lord his God out of the fish's belly, 2) And said, I cried by reason of mine affliction unto the Lord, and he heard me; out of the belly of hell (sheol) cried I, and thou heardest my voice.   *Jonah 2:1-2*
Be careful (anxious) for nothing; but in every thing by prayer and supplication with thanksgiving let your requests be made known unto God. 7) And the peace of God, which passeth all understanding, shall keep your hearts and minds through Christ Jesus.   *Philippians 4:6-7*

You may recall that our journey with Jonah began when the word of the Lord came to him telling him to go to Nineveh, that great city, and cry against it because their wickedness had come up before God. As we know, Jonah refused to do it. He took off in the other direction. Actually, Jonah is the only prophet in the Bible who is known to have openly defied or deliberately disregarded the word of God. Most of the other prophets, like Elisha and Isaiah, went and immediately did whatever it was that God had told them to do.

EXCUSES, EXCUSES, EXCUSES

Now, certain prophets may have pleaded with God, like Moses did when God told him to go to Pharaoh on behalf of the children of Israel to bring them forth out of Egypt, the land of their enslavement. Moses made every effort to talk his way out of what God had commissioned him to do. He told God, in Exodus 3:11, *"Who am I, that I should go unto Pharaoh, and that I should bring forth the children of Israel out of Egypt?"* But God assured Moses, in Exodus 3:12, *"Certainly I will be with thee; and this shall be a token unto thee, that I have sent thee..."* And God instructed Moses to throw his rod on the ground and, when he did, it turned into a large venomous snake. When Moses saw that, he took off running in the other direction, and I don't blame him. Had I seen a rod turn into a snake, I would have run away, too.

I remember, one day, I came home from work and found my wife and kids screaming and crying. I asked them, "What is going on?" They yelled, "There is a rattle snake in the garage!" I replied in disbelief, "A rattle snake?!" They screamed, "Yes, a big rattle snake!!" So, I grabbed my trusty baseball bat and went outside to the garage, but I did not see anything. Then, as I started walking to the side of the garage, I saw the large rattle snake. (Looking back now, it could have been a harmless bull snake but, at the time, we were convinced it was a rattle snake.)

When I first saw the snake, I jumped back. My wife and kids were trailing right behind me, so they saw it too. And one of them let out a scream. At least, I hope it was one of them. Maybe it was I who screamed. All I know is somebody screamed, and it sounds better for me to say they were doing all of the screaming. I admit we all ran, though, and I am sure the snake and I startled each other.

After a minute or two of pure panic, I told myself, "Calm down! Your wife and kids are watching you, and they're counting on you to kill that rattle snake."

So, I took a deep breath and crept up to the snake. I clasped the baseball bat and swung at the snake with all my might. The snake jumped and I did, too, but I managed to hit the snake mid-body. The snake drew back and jumped again, and I swung again and again and again. I did not kill the snake, but I did hit him a couple of times and I think he was hurt.

The snake retreated under a bush, and I tried to get at him but I could not. Finally, the snake slithered away. I decided he was no longer a threat, so we all calmed down. And my wife and kids congratulated me for being such a great hero. But, the truth is I was shaken to my core, in a full sweat, and relieved that the snake decided to go away. So, as a result of my personal encounter with a snake, I can appreciate Moses running away from the rod after it turned into a snake. Actually, had my wife and kids not been there, I would have gone in the house and left that snake alone.

Getting back to Moses, God told him to grab the serpent by the tail, which he did, and it became a rod again. I am not sure that I could have grabbed the rattle snake that was by our garage by the tail. However, I guess if God had told me to or if my wife and kids were in danger, I would have grabbed the snake. (Though, I realize I am not a great prophet and leader like Moses; I am just a husband and father.) God then told Moses to use the rod turning to a snake and back to a rod again as a sign so that the children of Israel would believe the Lord God of their fathers, the God of Abraham, Isaac, and Jacob, had appeared unto him.

Despite God's assurance to Moses through His divine signs, Moses still did not want to do what God had appointed him to do. Thus, when Moses' first excuse failed to change God's mind about sending him to Pharaoh, Moses proceeded to make several other excuses. "I have nothing to work with." "I do not speak well." "I am a 'nobody', and the children of Israel will not listen to me." "…Okay, if I go, who should I say sent me?"

God responded to Moses' question of "What should I say is the name of Him that has sent me?" with the all-defining phrase "I AM THAT I AM… has sent you to them," (Exodus 3:13-14). God identified Himself by Himself. God was saying, "I AM the Self-Existent One. I AM the eternal I AM. I AM the Creator of heaven and earth. I created every living creature, including the human beings you will face. I AM the everywhere present God. I AM the God "Who" keeps His promises. I AM able to do all that I

81

say I will do. I AM the God "Who" will set the children of Israel free. I AM able to supply all your need. Moses, you tell anyone that asks you, 'I AM that I AM sent me to you.'"

The phrase, "I AM that I AM", not only applies to Moses, but it also applies to you and me. Only, now, we do not have to say, "I AM that I AM sent me," because we know that Jesus is the great I AM. Jesus is the prince of peace. Jesus is the great, eternal wonder and holy counselor. Therefore, we can say, "Jesus sent me. Jesus saved me. Jesus healed, delivered, and set me free. Jesus is my key to living a life of victory." God went on to tell Moses to use the rod that was in his hand to stand against Pharaoh's magicians. God then told Moses that his brother Aaron would be a mouthpiece for him. Every excuse that Moses made, God had an answer for it. God had a solution to every problem that Moses posed. Therefore, Moses' confidence grew because he then knew that God would see him through. So, Moses went to Pharaoh and did all which God told him to do.

Jonah, on the other hand, did not question or debate with God. Jonah simply did not do what God told him to do. Jonah decided to disobey God and run away. But, Jonah was silly to think that he could have escaped God's presence.

What did David say in the 139th Psalm verses 7-10? *Whither shall I go from thy spirit? Or whither shall I flee from thy presence? If I ascend up into heaven, thou art there: If I make my bed in hell, behold, thou art there. If I take the wings of the morning, and dwell in the uttermost parts of the sea; Even there shall thy hand lead me, and thy right hand shall hold me.*

No matter where you go, God is leading, directing, and guiding your steps. Even when you do not think so, God is leading you in the direction that you should go. God is guiding you. You are where you are in life right now because God closed some doors and opened others for you. Not only is God leading and guiding you, but God also holds you. God comforts and keeps you securely and safely in His arms. So, do not be like Jonah and try to run away from God's presence. Rather, enter into His presence, as Psalm 100:4-5 exhorts, *Enter into his gates with thanksgiving, and into his courts with praise: be thankful unto him, and bless his name. For the Lord is good; his mercy is everlasting; and his truth endureth to all generations.*

PEACE – FRAGILE; HANDLE WITH CARE

Now, I admit that Jonah's actions really puzzled me. I mean, I would like to think that if the word of the Lord came to me, I would obey it right away. Maybe I would question it, like Peter did when he saw Jesus walking on the water and asked, "Is it you, Lord?" We all have seen people say that God told them something and He clearly did not, like the aforementioned preacher who said that the world was coming to an end in May, 2011 but, of course, it did not. Therefore, I would want to be sure that I was not delusional or imagining anything if God were to instruct me to do something.

Perhaps, I would be like Moses and ask God, "Are you sure "You" want me?" Moses had murdered someone, so he did not think he was worthy of God using him. And, although I have never done anything of that magnitude, I would feel unworthy like Moses did and question God, as well, saying, "Lord, are "You" sure that I am the one "You" want to do this?" I mean, let's face it. There are a whole lot of people who are more popular, more experienced, more talented, and better suited to this task than I. This church has twenty ministers in it, and I am number 20.

So, why in the world would you call on me or want me to do anything but read a scripture on 5th Sundays?" Yes, I would question God to see whether or not I had gotten the message straight. I would want to know if it were God Who was speaking to me, or was it the Chinese food with red hot chili peppers that I had eaten the night before. However, I do not believe that I would just run away like Jonah did.

Therefore, in order to understand Jonah's behavior better, I began to study Jonah more closely. It turns out that Jonah's name means "dove". In the New Testament, the dove was used to represent the Holy Spirit descending on Jesus Christ at his baptism. In the Old Testament, the dove was a symbol of peace, tranquility, and safety. For example, when Noah sent a dove out to find dry land after the flood, and the dove returned with an olive branch in its mouth, it marked that the waters had abated and habitable land existed. Since the *Book of Jonah* is found in the Old Testament, we can conclude that Jonah's name signifies a "dove of peace". Now, we know that peace is precious, but it can also be very fragile. As we have seen in the daily news, the peace between two countries, which may have taken years to establish, can break down in a matter of mere months. Peace can break down over money, debt, or a simple misunderstanding, misreading, or misinterpreting of information. The peace between two cities or two schools can break down over zoning laws, taxes, curfew, or the outcome of a football or basketball game. And, all too often, the peace between brothers and sisters can break down over almost anything. The kids could be sitting quietly watching television when, suddenly, one of them yells out, "Mommy, he hit me!" The other defends, "Well she was bothering me! She was making a lot of noise, and I could not hear the television."

And how fragile is the peace between in-laws? Your family may complain that your spouse has an attitude problem or bad manners because he (or she) acted like he did not want to speak. Or a family member may say, "How come your husband (or wife) did not eat our food? Was our food not good enough for him? I know I can cook, so what is his problem?" Or your family may say "Are you sure you want to marry into his family? They act too stiff [or too wild, too city, or too country]?"

Need I mention the peace between husbands and wives? Something as simple as a look can be interpreted as an act of war: "I see you. Who are you looking at like that?" And do not bother to make a tired excuse. You are probably better off keeping quiet. In fact, the peace between a husband and wife can be interrupted even when they are looking at the same thing. For example, they can watch a movie together and interpret it very differently from each other. Maybe the wife saw the hero's silence as a sign that he was too overcome with emotion to speak. But, the husband saw the hero's silence as him concentrating on how he was going to kill the bad guys. Then, after the movie is over and they discuss the picture, they cannot believe how drastically their views differed. And they begin to wonder what else they might not be seeing eye-to-eye on. Moreover, along with marriage, goes the matter of disappointments and setbacks. If a husband and wife are not careful, they can easily view any failures in their personal, professional, or married lives as their spouses fault: "Why couldn't you have been nicer to my boss? I did not get the raise or promotion because you never support me."

Truly, peace can be very fragile, and I believe that the peace Jonah had was also very fragile. Jonah may have appeared to have it all together on the outside. After all, Jonah was a prophet, a preacher, and a man of God. Surely, Jonah's dress, speech, demeanor, and occupation indicated that he was at peace with God, his fellow man, and himself. In addition, Jonah's father's name was Amittai, which means "true". Thus, Jonah was sometimes called the "son of truth". Come to think of it, all Christians should be called the "children of truth" because Jesus is the way, the *truth*, and the life. As Christians, we claim to be Christ like, so we all should be truthful like Christ, right?

THE PERFECT STORM

So, on the outside, Jonah appeared to be strong in the Lord. However, on the inside, Jonah was not as confident and peaceful as he seemed. Jonah was probably a real prayer warrior. I am sure that many of Jonah's prayers were answered. I imagine that when Jonah prayed for someone, God answered his prayers right away. But maybe, just maybe, when Jonah prayed for himself, God did not answer him exactly how or when he would have liked. Thus, although Jonah may have had the external appearance of being steady, secure, and peaceful, in actuality, Jonah was likely being tossed and blown about in emotional inner turmoil.

More than likely, Jonah was a perfectionist. Perfectionists are people who want everything to be just right. We all know people like that. In fact, one of them might be you. The perfectionist works hard to keep up appearances. She (or he) wants to make everyone think she has everything under control. The perfectionist drives the right car, keeps her home immaculately clean, and her kids are always well-groomed and straight "A" students. The perfectionist has the right spouse (or wants people to think she does), and she is known on her job, at her church, and in her community as being the one who can get things done.

Yet, inwardly, the perfectionist's stomach is churning. At night, she grinds her teeth. She often gets headaches because she feels the peace she has is so fragile that it could crumble at any time. She often dreads, in the recesses of her mind, that something bad will happen. She may not be able to put her finger on it, but she just feels certain that some misfortune lurks around the corner waiting to catch her off guard. She supposes she is just one mistake from being discovered as inadequate, one mere misstep from being revealed as less than perfect. For her, any gusty change, any minor turbulence, any windy disturbance in her life will cause her perfect image to be whisked away, and her fragile peace along with it.

Say, for instance, her co-worker behaves strangely toward her, or her boss speaks harshly to her. Maybe, the boss tells her that she did not do a project exactly the way he wanted it done. Still worse, the boss tells her this in front of everyone that she works with. Or perhaps, she does not like the way her spouse paid attention to an attractive, young woman. Or maybe, she has been dating the same guy for six years, and then he breaks up with her and plans to marry someone else he has been dating for only six months.

Now, one might respond to a co-worker's indifferent attitude by thinking, "I know she is going through some tough times right now. Normally, we get along just fine. So, I am sure my co-worker does not have anything personally against me." Moreover, one might choose to handle the boss' criticism of the completed assignment calmly, reassuring herself, "I performed my duty to the best of my ability. The boss is under a lot of pressure, and he must be having a bad day." In addition, one might address the scenario of a seemingly flirtatious spouse by saying, "I know you did not mean anything by holding the door open and saying 'hello' to her. You were just being polite. I know you love me." And one might regard her ex-boyfriend's sudden engagement to another woman with wise, well-wishing words, such as, "I am glad for the time we had together. I learned a lot about myself, and I guess I helped him reach the point where he could become a good husband to someone else."

Then, there are those with combative or confrontational personalities. These people, when faced with the same situations, often will get mad and fight back. For example, a person like this might react to the co-worker with an argumentative attitude, saying, "I don't know why you're acting funny. You are not all that, and in two minutes you are going to need my help." Moreover, this personality type might become defensive against her critical boss regarding her questionable performance on the project with words like, "I did this project and the last two assignments better than you or anyone else could ever hope to do it!" I imagine she then would storm out, not caring that she has jeopardized her job for talking back to her boss.

Still, such a one might retaliate against her seemingly flirtatious spouse with her own story: "You think you're so cute, huh? Well, a week ago when I was coming out of Starbucks, a man in a Mercedes Benz asked me for my phone number. I just do not tell you every time somebody flirts with me or tells me that I'm pretty. So, go ahead and flirt if you want because I can flirt, too." Finally, the confrontational or combative type with the boyfriend that dumps her and quickly becomes engaged to marry someone else might react with anger. She might spend the night sitting in front of his house in her parked car hoping to see him and stop the wedding. Or, worse, she might key his car or slash his tires, thinking, "Nobody plays me or wastes my time and gets away with it."

And of course, there are those who seem to let things go. They never seem to get their feathers ruffled, and they face life's challenges with what seems to be great patience and calm. However, for perfectionists, for people like Jonah, any of the above-mentioned scenarios could send them into a downward spiral of self-doubt, isolation, and despair. In other words, some people would allow similar circumstances to lead them into depression.

TODAY'S COMMON COLD

I read in a dental journal that 20% of all U.S. citizens, between the ages of eighteen and eighty, suffer with major bouts of depression. This stands to reason because this age range represents our working years. In today's economy, our jobs are no longer very secure. It seems that companies get bought out, downsized, closed up, or moved away almost overnight. One can show up for work on Monday morning and, by Monday evening, return home unemployed. Somehow, even those with high-paying jobs often barely have enough money to make ends meet.

This is also the time in which we are having and raising children. And, as parents, we are never quite sure if we are doing enough for them or doing too much for them. Unfortunately, kids do not come with blue prints. What works with rearing one child may not work with rearing another. What worked well with bringing up the kids in your family may not work at all with bringing up the kids in someone else's family.

In addition, this age range encompasses the marrying years. Many people are working on their second and third marriages. And oftentimes, someone who has never been married before will get involved with someone who has been married and divorced several times. Quite commonly, a person with no children will enter a relationship with someone who has children from two or three previous relationships. And, all too often, both people in the relationship already have their own children.

Thus, blended-family issues arise, such as, how will step parenting be handled; when and where will visitations occur, and from whom and to what extent will the child be disciplined, to name only a few.

This is also the time of life when we must face the difficult reality of aging parents. "Who will take care of them?", "Where will they live?", and "How will we pay for it?" are questions which frequently arise, especially concerning parents who are sickly or senile. Thus, with all of the pressures facing people between the ages of eighteen and eighty, it is no small wonder that depression is considered "the common cold of mental health" for the 21st century.

One might say depression is the natural response to a loss. For example, the loss of a loved one, a spouse, a child, a parent, a sibling, or a friend could cause a momentary bout of depression. Even the loss of a job, a frequent occurrence in today's economy, which might easily result in the loss of a home and the eventual loss of a marriage, could be a recipe for depression. And certainly, failed health or the disappointment of failed dreams, goals, and visions all could lead to depressed periods in one's life.

Suppose that a person had the dream of becoming a star athlete but never got off the bench. Or someone wanted to go to medical or law school but never got accepted. Perhaps, one envisioned herself married by age thirty, but age forty has come and gone; yet, there is no Mr. Right in sight. Maybe, one planned to have children but never could conceive; meanwhile, there are women who don't even want kids that seem to get pregnant without trying. All of these scenarios potentially trigger bouts of depression.

Depression can be likened to a computer, which becomes overloaded and freezes up. The computer needs to shut down and reboot, so the computer will turn itself off. Then, after a few minutes, the computer will indicate that it is ready to start up again, and it will function just fine. The same goes for depression regarding one's mind. Normal depression helps one to slow down and to process what has been lost, allowing one time to adjust and, then, start up again. However, for a perfectionist like Jonah, normal depression is not enough. This type of person often slides into a deep depression that is hard to shake in just a couple of weeks.

Now, I know some may ask, "How do you know that Jonah was depressed?" To that I respond, "Just look at how Jonah behaved." Jonah acted like a depressed person. People who are depressed tend to interpret everything in a negative way. For instance, when God told Jonah to go to Nineveh and cry against it, instead of Jonah seeing that the Lord was giving him a golden opportunity to preach the word and possibly save an entire city, Jonah interpreted God's command as a potential source of embarrassment and failure.

Jonah had convinced himself that the city would never change and that God would spare them anyway. ***And God saw their works, that they turned from their evil way; and God repented of the evil, that he said that he would do unto them; and he did it not. But it displeased Jonah exceedingly, and he was very angry*** (Jonah 3:10-4:1). Jonah became angry because he thought that he would be labeled as a false prophet. Rather than seeing his assignment as an opportunity to share God's mercy and grace to over one million people, Jonah managed to view his commission from God as a total negative.

Some, scholars say that Jonah wanted Nineveh destroyed because it would have served as an example to the children of Israel of what would happen to them had they kept on disobeying God. In other words, they hold that Jonah wanted to use the destruction of Nineveh to scare Israel into acting right towards God. However, I think that acting to ensure the death of over a million people would have been a pretty negative thing for Jonah to have done. However, Jonah never made any direct reference to Israel throughout his entire book, so I do not believe concern for Israel was Jonah's priority.

What we do know is that Jonah ran away. Jonah tried to evade the situation completely. *But Jonah rose up to flee unto Tarshish from the presence of the Lord, and went down to Joppa; and he found a ship going to Tarshish: so he paid the fare thereof, and went down into it… …But Jonah was gone down into the sides of the ship; and he lay, and was fast asleep* (Jonah 1:3,5). And not only did Jonah run, but he also managed to sleep through what, for others, was a sleepless situation.

Isn't that what depressed people do – sleep a lot? Admittedly, not all depressed people sleep a lot. Some depressed people have trouble falling asleep or cannot sleep through the night. Their minds are so actively wandering and worrying about what they have lost or what they think they might lose, that they can hardly relax enough to sleep. In general, though, depressed people sleep a lot, often for fourteen to sixteen hours at a time. They may wake up just long enough to get the kids off to school, etc. Then, they return back to their escape of sleep until it is time to pick the kids up and bring them back home.

So, Jonah got onto the boat and went fast asleep. *But the Lord sent out a great wind into the sea, and there was a mighty tempest [or storm] in the sea, so that the ship was [in danger of being] broken [in two]* (Jonah 1:4). And, still, Jonah slept. He did not toss and turn or lie half awake, staring at the ceiling. Jonah was out cold. Jonah slept until the captain of the ship woke him up, saying, "How can you sleep through such a terrible storm?" But, the shipmaster did not understand that Jonah was depressed and was trying to reboot because he simply could not handle what was going on in his life. As far as Jonah was concerned, when it rains it pours, and the storm was just another bad thing that was happening to him.

Once the shipmaster had awakened Jonah, Jonah told the sailors, in Chapter 1 verse 12 *...Take me up, and cast me forth into the sea; so shall the sea be calm [for] you: for I know that for my sake this great tempest is upon you.* But the sailors did not want to do it. Maybe, there was something about Jonah's appearance, demeanor, speech, or dress that made the sailors suspicious of his request. Or maybe, Jonah waking up and suggesting that he be thrown overboard caused the sailors to surmise that Jonah was not thinking straight and must have been depressed. Thus, as we discussed in **Chapter 3: God Has Prepared a Place for You**, the sailors rowed even harder but could not overcome the storm. Finally, after seeing that their efforts, though valiant, were futile, they begged God not to hold Jonah's life against them, and they threw him overboard. *And the sea ceased from her raging* (Jonah 1:15b). The sea immediately became calm, and the sailors were able to complete their journey.

GOD'S CURE FOR DEPRESSION

Now the Lord had prepared a great fish to swallow up Jonah (Jonah 1:17a). When Jonah told the sailors to throw him overboard, he had no idea a great fish was lurking nearby; nor did Jonah know the fish would swallow him whole. Jonah had imagined that, once the sailors threw him overboard, it would be all over for him. But, little did Jonah know the Lord had prepared a place for him. *And Jonah was in the belly of the fish three days and three nights* (Jonah 1:17b). The Lord prepared a place where Jonah could rest, a place where he could have the chance to shut down, reboot, repent, and get it together.

One could say that the time Jonah spent in the belly of the fish was like Jonah being in prison. Actually, prison is intended to offer an inmate the time to reflect, to repent, and to determine to change his (or her) attitude and behavior. This is not an implication that depressed people need to go to prison. However, therapists often suggest that their depressed patients go on retreat or to an institution in order to shut down and reboot. Of course, with these recommendations, therapists commonly prescribe a ton of medications to help their patients recover.

As believers, though, we can turn to the Lord because prayer is the key to full recovery from depression. When we feel depression creeping in, we should pray for the peace of God. That is what Jonah did. *[He] prayed unto the Lord his God out of the fish's belly, And said, I cried by reason of mine affliction unto the Lord, and he heard me; out of the belly of hell cried I, and thou heardest my voice* (Jonah 2:1-2).

Remember that, in Chapter 1 verse 6 of our text, the shipmaster told Jonah to pray when he found him sleeping at the bottom of the ship. But, the scripture does not indicate that Jonah prayed at that point. Once in the belly of the fish, remarkably, Jonah did decide to pray. That just goes to show that you can pray anywhere. The scripture exhorts that men (or people) should always pray. Wherever you are and whatever situation you find yourself in, you can pray. You can turn it over to Jesus, and he will make a way out of no way.

Jonah was trapped in the belly of the fish, but he was free to pray. Paul and Silas were locked in jail, but they had liberty to pray. They did not panic in their circumstance, but they prayed and God set them free. No matter what situation has you bound, prayer can turn it around. Prayer is the answer. Prayer is the key to having God hear you and set you free. No matter how bad you may feel, no matter what you have lost. Jesus paid for it all on the cross. Prayer is your cure for depression.

Apostle Paul said it this way in Philippians 4:6a, *Be [anxious] for nothing…* Yes, stuff happens. Yes, you suffer loss. No, things do not always work out the way you thought they would. And despite your best efforts, things do not always go as you planned. But, you must not become anxious over it. Do not become angry or depressed. Rather, as Apostle Paul encouraged, in everything and in every situation that upsets you – your job or loss of a job; your marriage, your relationship, or lost love; your children, family, or friends; loneliness; financial struggles; or, sickness – in everything, in every single thing, pray and trust God.

The pursuit of perfection is an admirable goal. We all should strive to be like Christ. But, we are not Christ. We are not perfect. Jesus admonished the accusers of the woman caught in the very act of adultery that only the one who was without sin should cast the first stone of her punishment. And no one picked up so much as a pebble; they all just walked away. Jesus, who is perfect, would not even condemn the woman, but rather, told her to go and to sin no more. The blood of Jesus covers a multitude of sins. This does not mean we should practice sin, absolutely not. However, we are human, and as such, we make mistakes.

But, we must not dwell on our mistakes or worry about what others will think and say. The truth is those same people who we have been worried would find out about our mistakes are just as concerned that we may discover theirs. So, what we should focus on, whenever we fall short or fail, is praying, repenting, and asking God to help us not to fall again.

In addition, Apostle Paul instructed that we should pray with thanksgiving, that we should be thankful for what God has already given us. God has given us salvation, health, food to eat, air to breathe, and minds to think. Even when we think things could not get any worse, God is blessing us; God is keeping us; God is guiding us; and, God is protecting us.

Friend, remember this: Jesus promised that he would not leave you comfortless. So, God cares. No matter how depressed you get, God is not through with you, yet. You are not alone. All is not lost. Jesus died for you on the cross. You have a lot to be thankful for; you have a lot to be grateful for; and, you have a lot to praise Him for. Whatever situation you are facing is a momentary set back. I understand it is bad right now, but it is momentary. The sun will rise tomorrow and, in God's own time, He will relieve you of your sorrows. There is hope for tomorrow because ... ***Weeping may endure for a night, but joy cometh in the morning*** (Psalm 30:5b).

Apostle Paul said that when you pray with thanksgiving, you can ***...let your requests be made known unto God*** (Philippians 46b). The apostle was not suggesting that God has to be told about your needs, wants, or desires because

He knows all about your troubles. In fact, God knows what you really need before you even find the words to tell Him or ask Him for help. But, He wants you to pray to Him to show Him that you trust Him. Thus, prayer is the cure for your depression. God can and will deliver you. Pray, and God will hear you. When God hears your prayers, God will act to deliver you. Yes, at times, you may get depressed, but you do not have to stay that way. There is a cure for depression, and you will find it when you pray.

CHAPTER 5

GOD WILL REMEMBER YOU

A CLOSER LOOK AT DEPRESSION

Then Jonah prayed unto the Lord his God out of the fish's belly, 2) And said, I cried by reason of mine affliction unto the Lord, and he heard me; out of the belly of [sheol] cried I, and thou heardest my voice. 3) For thou hadst cast me into the deep, in the midst of the seas; and the floods compassed me about: all thy billows and thy waves passed over me. 4) Then I said, I am cast out of thy sight; yet I will look again toward thy holy temple. 5) The waters compassed me about, even to the soul: the depth closed me round about, the weeds were wrapped about my head. 6) I went down to the bottoms of the mountains; the earth with her bars was about me forever: yet hast thou brought up my life from corruption, O Lord my God. 7) When my soul fainted within me I remembered the Lord: and my prayer came in unto thee, into thine holy temple. 8) They that observe lying vanities forsake their own mercy. 9) But I will sacrifice unto thee with the voice of thanksgiving; I will pay that that I have vowed. Salvation is of the Lord. 10)

And the Lord spake unto the fish, and it vomited out Jonah upon the dry land.
Jonah 2:1-10

Jonah was quite a unique prophet in that he was the first one whom God had sent to prophesy to the Gentiles. All of Jonah's predecessors, like Prophets Isaiah, Daniel, and Ezekiel, delivered their messages of the Gentiles' impending fate to their own people, the children of Israel. Jonah was the first prophet to be given the responsibility of addressing the Gentiles directly, just as Apostles Peter and, especially, Paul would later be commissioned to do in the New Testament eras.

BEHIND MENTAL BARS

Jonah's blatant refusal to do so, however, led him on an unforgettable journey of unnecessary, self-inflicted drama, which, in turn, landed him in the belly of a great fish for three days and three nights. It was at this low point that Jonah finally decided to pray, saying*... I cried by reason of mine affliction unto the Lord...* (Jonah 1:2). "I cried to the Lord," Jonah was saying, "because of my pain and suffering." Recall from **Chapter 4: God's Cure For Depression** that Jonah failed to see the honor in his God-given assignment to *...go to Nineveh, that great city, and cry against*

it; [because] their wickedness [had]
come up before [God] (Jonah 1:1*).* Instead,
Jonah viewed being the first prophet sent to warn
the Gentiles as a type of demotion or source of
shame, as if he were no longer worthy of
prophesying to God's chosen people, the children
of Israel.

At the same time, Jonah felt an immense amount
of guilt. He knew he had not only selfishly
risked the lives of the sailors who had been so
kind to him during the raging tempest, but also
he had cost them their livelihood when they
threw their cargo overboard in attempt to save
their sinking ship. Jonah understood all too well
that, had he obeyed God in the first place or
confessed quickly that he was the one whom God
had sent the storm after, the sailors and their
cargo would not have been needlessly involved.

And like so many people do when they know
they are to blame for something, which they fail
to immediately resolve, Jonah replayed the
sequence of events over and over in the cinema
of his mind until he sank from the dark hole of
guilt into the gaping pit of depression. Jonah felt
he had lost his prestige and favor with the Lord,
his fellow prophets, the sailors, and himself. It
was there, in the belly of the fish, that Jonah
became convinced he had hit rock bottom.

107

To Jonah, the three dark days and three lonely nights trapped in the great fish's belly were a seemingly endless sentence in an abysmal, watery prison.

In verses 3 through 6 of our text, Jonah described his desperate conditions, saying … *For thou hadst cast me into the deep*… Jonah realized that the sailors were tools used by God to cast him into the sea or convict him of his offence. He went on to say …*all thy billows and waves passed over me.* He recognized that the wind and waves also had been employed by God in order to capture and punish him for his disobedience. *Then [Jonah] said, I am cast out of thy sight*… He began to fear that God had rejected him or "thrown the book at him" for his transgression. Moreover, Jonah's mental torment became so vivid that he literally saw *the weeds [that] were wrapped about [his] head* as inescapable prison bars, rather than mere seaweed the hungry fish happened to gulp down while swallowing him whole.

Jonah's inner turmoil stemmed from knowing that the mess which he had found himself entangled in all could have been avoided had he done what the Lord had instructed him to do in the first place. And, for many, this feeling is all too familiar. Let's say, for example, you are a woman, and you find yourself involved with a married man who promises you he will leave his wife. But, somehow, you find out he is still actively seeing her. Now you have proof that he is no good and just wasting your time; yet, you feel you love him too much to leave him.

Perhaps, instead, you are a woman who has been dating the same man for several years. You do everything for him that a wife would – you cook for him, clean for him, make love to him, and bear and care for his children – yet, for the life of you, you cannot conceive why he will not marry you. Still worse, he does not seem to be thinking about marriage because the topic only arises when you mention it.

Or, maybe, there is some family drama, which you know you should stay out of; still, the family manages to suck you right into the middle of it. Now, family members are angry with you for something that never even concerned you in the first place. Certainly, any one of these scenarios could leave you feeling tangled in a web of confusion, guilt, anger, and depression. But, the most difficult pill to swallow in each of these cases is in knowing the drama you have been facing could easily have been avoided had you first done what you knew was right.

An objective observer, therapist, counselor, pastor, friend, and your own conscience would remind you that all of these problems have simple solutions. First, one should *never* get involved with a married person, *period.* Secondly, if someone takes more than two years to ask you to marry them, you are probably wasting your time. That is not to say that couples, which date longer than two years, never marry. However, I think most men know right away if the woman he has been courting is "the one".

After all, ladies, would you take six years to buy a dress? Would you keep going back to the department store, as often as you please, just to try it on for size or to see if the dress still fits? Then, after six years have passed, would you finally say, "Okay, I guess I will buy it." No! First of all, a wise store owner would not allow you to keep coming around, trying on the same dress without making a purchase. Secondly, if you have to go through all of that in order to buy a dress, chances are you really do not want it or there is something about that particular one – perhaps the price, style, fit, etc., – which you find unsuitable for you.

Thus, anyone observing a person in any of these situations would simply say, "Get out. It's that simple. Get yourself out of that mess." To the involved individual, however, such sound advice may not be quite so clear-cut because, in the person's heart and mind, she feels completely cornered with no way out that would lead to a happy ending. And therein we find the common conundrum because the toughest battles we fight and the most challenging struggles we face in life are often those which we encounter in our hearts and minds.

Embarrassment, guilt, anger, frustration, loneliness, desperation, and depression are all issues which meet us on a mental and emotional plane. And these inward dilemmas are so real to the person who must combat them that they can produce actual physiological symptoms. Anxiety, nervousness, sweating, high blood pressure, stroke, upset stomach, diarrhea, headaches, and lethargy represent just a short list of physical manifestations, which commonly arise from one's internal conflict.

Moreover, the powerful effects of these thoughts and feelings could easily drive a person down the lonely road of depression – that feeling of hopelessness, listlessness, and despair usually associated with a loss. And, as we have discussed in the previous chapter, depression can result from the loss of almost anything, even the loss of something trivial. One can misplace a favorite hat or a pair of designer sunglasses, and it can be enough to trigger a momentary depression. Losing one's car keys can cause one to think, "Nothing ever goes right for me. Why do things always happen to me? Life is so unfair. I am so unlucky."

SOMEONE TO TALK T0

Unfortunately, apart from this type of negative "why me?", "I'm such a loser" self-talk, depressed people rarely dialogue about their difficulties to anyone else. Rarely, does one hear a truly depressed person say, "Hey, I am depressed, and I need someone to talk to about what is troubling me." Instead, people who are depressed often hide behind a smoke screen of complaints regarding any and everything, except their root problems.

For example, they may go to doctors, complaining of back aches, tooth aches, stomach aches, or headaches. Some may even sight trouble sleeping. Additionally, depressed people may gripe to their pastors and friends about their marriages or relationships with statements like,

"She no longer meets my needs. The sex is boring, and she just doesn't excite me anymore;" or "He's so insensitive. I am so tired from work, the kids, cooking, and cleaning that I just lay there, hoping he gets it over with quickly so I can get some sleep."

Moreover, depressed single women may grumble that "there are no good men anymore" and that "all men want, nowadays, is sex without a commitment." They may then add, "If I make him wait too long for sex; he leaves. But, if I give in too soon; he leaves anyway." Then there are those with depression who often cry, "How come I fast and pray, and God still does not answer me;" or "If God does give me what I prayed for, it never seems to work out like I thought it would."

Since those who suffer from depression do not usually ask for help, friends or family members often suggest that the individual seek professional counsel. Sometimes, the mere act of talking openly to an attentive person about ones problems is helpful in lifting a person out of a depressed state. That a professional counselor frequently is an unfamiliar or impartial third party is a fact that also proves helpful in cases where the depressed person attributes a great deal of his (or her) life's woes to the same family and friends, which recommend he seeks help.

On the other hand, there are those with depression who will discuss what is bothering them to anyone and everyone who will listen. But, of course, such constant whining is counterproductive and serves to prolong the depressed state. And, let's face it, people who do nothing but constantly grouse about how miserable they feel quickly become ostracized from family and friends because no one wants to be around negativity all the time.

Finally, there are those, like Jonah, who find themselves completely alone, with no one to talk to. Jonah was by himself in the belly of the fish, and that is how we sometimes may feel when faced with adversity. There really are times in our lives when we feel there is no one to whom we can turn, no one who will truly hear and understand us without judging.

And it is at times like these that we may feel as though we have hit rock bottom, as Jonah described when he bellowed, **I went down to the bottoms of the mountains; the earth with her bars were about me forever** (Jonah 2:6a).

In the belly of the fish, surrounded by water, entangled in seaweed, at the base of the sea, Jonah truly had no one to talk to. He was left with no one and nothing but his regret. And it was there, at his lowest point, where his very soul began to ache. His soul agonized with emotion over his series of unwise choices, which had led him to such a pass, and it writhed from the pain of having to admit that he had been the culprit of his perilous predicament.

PIG PEN EXPERIENCE

This "soul ache", which Jonah felt, resembles what the prodigal son, in Luke 15:11-32, experienced when he had squandered his inheritance. To briefly summarize the scripture passage, the younger of a rich man's two sons asked his father for his inheritance. Upon receiving it, the young son went to another country and foolishly spent all of his fortune on wine, women, and song. (I mean, this guy partied like he had won the lottery.)

And when he had spent all, there arose a mighty famine in that land; and he began to be in want (Luke 15:14). So, the young man got a job tending pigs, *and he would fain have filled his belly with the husks that the swine did eat* (Luke 15:16a). The young man had sunken so low that he was willing to eat the scraps, husks, apple cores, and orange and banana peels, which the pigs ate. *And no man gave unto him* (Luke 15:16b). It is funny how, when a man's fortune runs out, his friends, fame, and women often run out, too.

Thus, the young man's soul did ache for knowing that he had hit rock bottom and had lost all of his riches at the hand of his own poor choices. There he was, an heir of a wealthy, well-respected man; yet, he had been reduced to filling his belly with the same slop, which he fed the pigs he tended for survival, all because he had chosen to be wasteful. I can imagine him sitting down in the muck and mire, surrounded by the stench and squeal of swine, saying to himself, "This is the lowest I could possibly go. How could I have come to such a pass? The pigs are happy, playing, and eating. And I am stuck here in their pen having to take care of them and eat their crap 'cause no one who was there to help me spend my money is here for me now!!" The prodigal son was having the premiere pig pen experience.

During a pig pen experience, it is amazing what one will find appealing when the circumstances look desperate enough. I work in a prison where I have seen well-educated women, such as nurses, dental assistants, and even a dentist, fall in love with inmates. Inmates earn thirty five cents per hour while in prison and, upon their release, usually have job prospects that amount to next to zero. Additionally, many of the inmates have had sex with other inmates, either by choice or by force. Yet, some attractive, accomplished women become so lonely, so desperate for male companionship, that the convicts start to look good to them. In fact, I actually know of a female dentist who married an inmate.

Like the prodigal son, Peter also had a pig pen experience. Peter was one of Jesus Christ's most prominent, bold, and out-spoken disciples. It was Peter who walked on the water with Jesus. It was Peter who fist proclaimed that Jesus was the Christ, the Son of the living God. It was Peter whom Jesus blessed and gave the keys of the kingdom of heaven. And when Judas came, along with soldiers, priests, and Pharisees, to betray Jesus with a kiss, it was Peter who drew his sword to defend Jesus and cut off the ear of the high priest's servant.

Furthermore, we see in Matthew 26:31-35, ***Then saith Jesus unto [Peter and the other disciples], All ye shall be offended because of me this night: for it is written, I will smite the shepherd, and the sheep of the flock shall be scattered abroad. ...Peter answered and said unto him, Though all men shall be offended because of thee, yet will I never be offended. Jesus said unto him, Verily I say unto thee, That this night, before the cock crow, thou shalt deny me thrice. Peter said unto him, Though I should die with thee, yet will I not deny thee. Likewise also said all the disciples.***

Peter was adamant in telling Jesus Christ that he would never be too embarrassed or afraid to identify with and stand up for him. Peter went on to insist that he would be willing to die with Jesus. But, Jesus informed Peter that he would deny him not only once, but three times.

Let us continue Peter's story from Matthew 26:69-75, which reads as thus: *Now Peter sat [outside] in the palace [courtyard]: and a damsel came unto him, saying, Thou also [was] with Jesus of Galilee. But he denied before them all, saying, I know not what thou sayest. And when he was gone out into the porch, another maid saw him, and said unto them that were there, This fellow also was with Jesus of Nazareth. And again he denied with an oath, I do not know the man. And after a while came unto him they that stood by, and said to Peter, Surely thou also art one of them; for thy speech [gives thee away]. Then began he to curse and to swear, saying, I know not the man. And immediately the cock crew. And Peter remembered the word of Jesus, which said unto him, Before the cock crow, thou shalt deny me thrice. And he went out, and wept bitterly.*

So, Peter, the fisherman; Peter, the husband; Peter, the rough, tough, bold, sword-wielding, keys-to-the-kingdom-having, water-walking

118

disciple of Jesus Christ had his very own pig pen experience. He had sunk so low as to do that which he swore he would never do – deny his Savior and Lord. So, Peter wept bitterly because his own self-image had been completely shattered. See, we men mostly view ourselves as action heroes. Maybe we do not consider ourselves to be iron men, spider men, or supermen, but most of us tend to liken ourselves to the big-screen images of Arnold Schwarzenegger, Bruce Willis, Will Smith, or Denzel Washington. We think of ourselves as real men who would stand up for truth and justice, who would help the defenseless and innocent, and who would rise to the occasion whenever the need arose.

Peter viewed himself like this, and he swore that, as a real man and true disciple, he would never deny Jesus Christ. Remember, Peter had faith enough to step out of a boat into a stormy sea and walk on the water. So, surely, Peter felt that he would have faith enough to face Jesus Christ's enemies. Yet, when the moment of truth came, Peter buckled. He just could not do it. He got scared, he chickened out, and he denied Christ. To add insult to injury, he could not hide or prevent people from associating him with Jesus Christ. Peter was in the courtyard, and a girl remembered he had been with Jesus Christ. He then went outside, and another girl declared she had seen him with Jesus Christ. Later, a group of people standing nearby recognized that he spoke as though he had been with Jesus Christ. However, because Peter did not want to be arrested, punished, or killed, he vehemently denied his fellowship with Jesus Christ all three times.

I would imagine each time Peter denied Jesus Christ he felt a piece of himself fall away. Peter's shoulders probably began to droop and he must have stood a little shorter because, in his own eyes, he had lost his stature or self-respect. See, generally, for men, self-respect and the respect of others are more important than being loved. Even scripture tells women to *honor* their husbands, while instructing men to love their wives (Ephesians 5:33). Thus, once Peter realized he had denied his Savior, which he swore emphatically he would never do, he felt reduced to a weaker, inferior version of himself. In fact, Peter wept so hard and for so long that one translation of scripture states his tears left permanent grooves in his face.

MY PERSONAL PIG PEN STORY

Unfortunately, I can relate to Peter's feeling of total self-disappointment because I, too, had my own pig pen experience once upon a time. Prior to my being happily married now, I was once, many years ago, married to someone else. To tell the truth, the marriage seemed doomed almost from the start. Somehow, we got off on the wrong foot. We started to argue, fuss, and fight on our honeymoon, and we never seemed to stop.

I did not know what was wrong or how to fix it. All I knew was my ego had been bruised because I had married her, and we were so unhappy. I was a dentist with my own practice and a Porsche 911 sports car, so a lot of women wanted to marry me. But there I was with the one woman I had chosen to marry, and she was not responding well to me at all. Thus, being the immature, insecure man that I was at that time, I retaliated by having affairs.

Now, when we first got married we lived in a multi-family house, which my father owned and rented out to me and a couple of other tenants. It was the year in which Jesse Jackson ran for president. (I remember actually meeting him when my church choir sang for him at a rally.) Anyway, on the night of the Democratic National Convention, Jesse Jackson was on the television giving a speech and was doing very well, so I called my mother. We talked to each other as we listened to him speak: "Don't be a jerk; we want work! Don't give us incarceration; we want education! Don't give us dope; we want hope! Keep hope alive! Keep hope alive! Keep hope alive!"

While I was on the phone with my mother, I thought my wife was in the kitchen cooking dinner but, as it turned out, she was not. Apparently, she thought it would be a good time to go through my wallet. (Back then, we did not commonly use cell phones, so people actually exchanged phone numbers.) And whenever I would get a woman's phone number, I would keep it in my wallet. Of course, I tried never to leave my wallet out of my sight. However, on that night I did. I think that I had worked out at the gym before I came home, so I must have showered, changed clothes, and put my wallet down, having been distracted by the Jesse Jackson speech and talking to my mother.

Suddenly, my wife came into the room screaming and yelling about me being a "no good, lying, cheating dog." I was caught completely off guard. She lunged at me with a pair of scissors. I managed to block the scissors from cutting my face, so she wound up stabbing me in the hand, which then bled a lot. Next, I grabbed her by her hair and yanked her down to the floor. She then proceeded to kick me and throw at me anything she could get her hands on – pots, pans, dishes, glasses, books, lamps, and even the iron. We yelled and screamed and chased each other. We made quite a ruckus.

She kept accusing me of cheating on her with the woman whose phone number she had found, but the truth is I did not know that particular woman. She had left her phone number on my car, and I just put it in my wallet. Now, to be completely honest, I probably would have cheated with her because I had certainly cheated on her with other women. But, at that moment, I had not yet even met that particular woman!

Well, with all of the chaos which had occurred, it is no small wonder that someone called the cops. It may have been one of the other tenants. (Though, now that I think about it, it may well have been my mother because I do not remember ever hanging up the phone.) So, the police rang the doorbell, and I answered the door. My shirt was torn and covered with blood, and my hand was still bleeding because I had not been able to tend to it since my wife was still trying to *kill* me. When my wife came to the door, she looked crazed and disheveled and started yelling to the police to lock my no good, lying, cheating behind up!

At that time in New Jersey, the law stated that whenever the police responded to a domestic disturbance, the male had to leave the premises. The male had to leave regardless of who started it or what happened during it. And, to prove that when it rains, it pours, one of the responding officers was a dental patient of mine. (I had a contract with the city to provide dental care for the police officers.) This particular officer liked to talk and joke a lot, so I had no doubt that he would tell everybody on the police force, "I had to remove Dr. Jackson from his home last night because his wife was trying to kill him. And it looked like she was winning!" I knew he would get a lot of laughs at my expense.

Now, although I was told to leave, I had refused to do so. After all, it was my father's house, and she had attacked me. The officers tried to be patient with me but, eventually, their patience ran out. The officers grabbed their night sticks and said, "Look doc, if you do not leave now, then we will make you leave." So, I took a deep breath – I think I was deciding whether I should resist them or not. Then, I exhaled, and as the air went out of my lungs, all of the fight went out of me, too. My wife had won. I was totally defeated.

The police let me get my car keys, and they made my wife give me my wallet. Then, they escorted me to my car, assuring me that they would not charge me with any offense. They did advise me to get a lawyer, though. I thanked them, drove off in my car, and stopped in front of an elementary school that was down the street. I got out of my car, sat on the curb, and began to cry. And I did not cry only a few tears. No. But, like Peter, I wept bitterly. I could not believe I had come to such a pass. I had graduated from Purdue University, where I played football in front of 70,000 people. (I am not saying that I was a star athlete because I was not. But, I went there and I played there.) Also, I had graduated from Howard Dental School and had bought my own private practice and my dream sports car. Until that point, I had always thought of myself as a nice guy. I had never used drugs, smoke, or drank. I had come from a godly family and had grown up in church.

But the truth finally hit me: Just because I had grown up in the church did not mean that the church, the love of God, had grown in me. I was not behaving in a godly manner and, though I thought I was a nice person, I had not been nice toward my own wife. I had blamed her for everything that went wrong in our marriage but, at that instant, upon me hitting rock bottom, it had become crystal clear that I had been the root cause of all of the turmoil in our marriage. My wife's bad behavior had been largely in response to my bad, selfish, and immature behavior.

Now, I hope that few people have behaved as poorly as I did; yet, I do believe that we all have done something we regret. We all have gone through some difficulty in our lives, and we all have, at least once, experienced a personal pig pen or soul-aching experience. At some point in this journey of life, we all have faced a period where we lost hope and felt down-trodden or despondent. Maybe, for some, it was a battle with alcoholism or drug-abuse. Others may have suffered rape or some form of abuse, maybe at an early age, which left its victims feeling helpless, confused, and desperately alone. Then there are those which had to face job loss, the loss of a home, or the loss of a marriage. And let's not forget those who have had challenges in the closely related areas of health and wealth. After all, the number one reason people go bankrupt in this country is because of medical bills. Remember, the Bible tells us when Job lost all of his wealth and health. His situation looked so bleak that his wife told him to curse God and die.

...EVEN YOU, JESUS?!

Little do many realize that even Jesus Christ had his own soul-aching, pig pen experience in the garden of Gethsemane, when he knew Judas was to betray him in order that he should suffer torture and crucifixion. So what did Jesus do? He prayed to the Father to remove "this bitter cup" or to take away his burden of sacrificing his perfect life to rescue an entire sinful world. As Mark 14:33-34 reads... ***And he taketh with him Peter and James and John, and began to be [greatly troubled], and to be [deeply distressed]; And saith unto them, My soul is exceeding sorrowful unto death: tarry ye here and watch.*** Do you see that? Jesus was depressed! Jesus Christ, the Son of God, the Messiah, the Prince of Peace, when faced with the onus of losing his life, became very depressed.

Luke also gives an account of Jesus praying in the garden of Gethsemane in Chapter 22 verse 44... ***And being in agony he prayed more earnestly: and his sweat was as it were great drops of blood falling down to the ground.*** Jesus had prayed so hard that he popped some blood vessels in his head and sweat blood. Jesus was not playing around; he was earnestly praying. He wanted to live. He was hoping for a reprieve similar to when Abraham (in Genesis

Chapter 22) was about to sacrifice his son Isaac in obedience to God but saw a ram in the bush, which he offered up instead. However, there was no ram in the bush for Jesus. So, he gave up his hope of being reprieved, and he faced the cross.

Jesus endured being wrongfully convicted, brutally beaten, and mercilessly mocked. Then, he was hung on the cross between two thieves, stabbed in his side, and left to die. Thus, would any one dare question why, in Matthew 27:46, *[At] about the ninth hour Jesus cried with a loud voice, saying, Eli, Eli, lama sabachthani? that is to say, MY GOD, MY GOD, WHY HAST THOU FORSAKEN ME?* Jesus felt totally abandoned and rejected because the weight and the punishment of all of humanity's sins were being executed upon him. He, who knew no sin, bore our sins on the cross (2 Corinthians 5:21). What love, what love, what kind of love was that? *Greater love hath no man than this, that a man lay down his life for his friends* (John 15:13).

And love is precisely the reason why God sent his Son Jesus into the world. As John Chapter 3 verses 17 and 16 read *... God sent not his Son into the world to condemn the world; but that the world through him might be saved. For God so loved the world, that he gave his only begotten Son, that whosoever believeth in him should not perish, but have everlasting life.*

God loved us despite our selfishness, disobedience, and sin. God loved us enough to have Jesus to suffer and to die on the cross, so we might have eternal life.

Make no mistake; Jesus did die. Jesus lay in the grave for three days, just as Jonah remained in the belly of the fish for three days. However, that is the point at which the parallel between Jesus and Jonah ends because, while Jonah suffered for his own sins, Jesus, who was without sin, actually died for the sins of the whole world. Oh, Satan, death, and the grave thought they had won; and, right now, your problem, situation, or circumstance may seem to have gotten the best of you. But hold on, have faith, and pray. Even if you become so overwhelmed with disappointment, that you feel yourself slipping into depression, please pray.

Remember that Jesus dying upon the cross is not where his story ended, and the trouble you are facing is not the end for you. It is not over for you. All is not lost. It will get better. I know it will get better for you because, on the third day, Jesus rose from the grave and declared all power in his hands. Jesus Christ has the power to save, heal, and deliver you. If you pray and turn your life, your worries, your embarrassment, your guilt, your shame, and your depression over to

Jesus, no matter how long you have been suffering and carrying your pain, Jesus will deliver you. He has not forgotten you.

To prove he has not forgotten you, consider this. On the morning that Jesus arose from the grave, women went to Jesus' sepulcher expecting to find his body. Instead, they found the stone, which should have been blocking the tomb's entrance, rolled away and an angel sitting inside the tomb, who said, *Be not [alarmed]: Ye seek Jesus of Nazareth, which was crucified; he is risen; he is not here; behold the place where they laid him. But go your way, tell his disciples and Peter that he goeth before you into Galilee...* (Mark 16: 6-7a). Notice, the angel instructed the women to tell the disciples *and Peter*. Even though Peter failed miserably and denied his Savior *three distinct times*; *still,* he was not forgotten. Jesus did not forget Peter, and He will not forget you.

Friend, you must know that there is no sin you can commit, there is no failure you can have, there is no loss you can suffer, and there is no emotional state you can slide into that will cause Jesus to forget about you. Apostle Paul phrased it best in Romans 8:35-39, when he penned, *"Who [or what] shall separate us from the love of Christ?" Shall tribulation, or distress, or*

persecution, or famine, or nakedness, or peril,
or sword? Nay [or No!]... For I am persuaded,
that neither death, nor life, nor angels, nor
principalities, nor powers, nor things present,
nor things to come, [N]or height, nor depth, nor
any other creature, shall be able to separate us
from the love of God, which is in Christ Jesus
our Lord.

That scripture assures me that nothing, absolutely
nothing – not your weakness, not your
immaturity, not your selfishness – nothing can
separate you from God's love for you. No matter
what you have done and no matter what has been
done to you, Jesus did not forget Peter and Jesus
will not forget you. Remember, if you get
thrown overboard, God is there. If you sink as
low as the bottom of the sea, God is there. If you
wind up in a pig pen, God is there. If you find
yourself under a pile of bills or in the pit of
sickness, God is there. Pray; do not wallow in
discouragement, depression, and despair. Pray
because only God can turn your situation around
and work it out for good. I know this because he
did the same for me.

GOD WILL REMEMBER YOU

Like the prodigal son, I had my pig pen experience because I was young and dumb. And, looking back, there are so many things that I used to say and do when I was young that I would never say or do now. Thankfully, in many ways, I grew up. As Apostle Paul said, in 1 Corinthians 13:11, ***When I was a child, I spake as a child, I understood as a child, I thought as a child: but when I became a man, I put away childish things.***   Believe it or not, if we live long enough, most of us do mature. The prodigal son certainly matured, as Luke 15:17 recounted *...**he came to himself...*** meaning he grew up. He recognized that he had acted foolishly and disrespectfully toward his father.

Moreover, Jonah had to mature and admit that his own disobedience was the root cause of his aching soul. Jonah had to grow up and confront that all the misfortune, which had befallen him – being caught in a tempest, thrown overboard, swallowed by a fish, tangled up in seaweed, and trapped at the bottom of the sea – was due to his own immaturity, selfishness, and disobedience. Yet, just as he had almost given up hope of being rescued, just as he had begun to slip into despair, like the prodigal son, he came to himself. He asserted, ***When my soul fainted within me I remembered the Lord*** (Jonah 2:7a).

Jonah remembered the Lord, and he remembered that the Lord also remembers. The Lord remembered Job suffering on a dung hill, and He turned his captivity and restored to him double of all that he had lost. The Lord remembered Joseph serving a senseless prison sentence, and He elevated him to the number two man in Egypt. The Lord remembered Daniel sitting in the lion's den, and He shut up the mouths of the ferocious beasts and delivered him from harm.

The Lord remembered all these and countless more, so why on earth would He not remember you?! Remember the Lord because He certainly remembers you. Your breakthrough, your turn around, your second chance, and your victory are just a matter of time. The Lord will remember you, and He will act on your behalf to deliver you. No matter how badly you may feel or how bleak your situation may appear, do not forget the One Who has not forgotten you.

Jonah came to himself and remembered the Lord, declaring, in Chapter 2 verse 9b, *Salvation [or deliverance] is of the Lord.* And that is when the Lord delivered Jonah. He rescued him by speaking *...unto the fish, and it vomited out Jonah upon the dry land* (verse 10). God set Jonah free – free from the sea, free from the fish, and free from the seaweed. Physically, emotionally, and spiritually, Jonah was set free, and God will do the same for you. Depression can have no hold on you once the Lord delivers you. Guilt and shame must release you when the Lord delivers you.

Like Jonah, I also remembered the Lord, and He did remember me. My previous marriage ended, but, to God be the glory, I was able to start over. I am now happily married, raising a godly family. And I know that what the Lord did for me, he surely can do for you. Whatever you are going through, wherever you are in your life's journey, and however you got there have no consequence on the power of Almighty God to rescue you. Just remember the Lord, and He will remember you, too.

CHAPTER 6

DOES DOING WELL DISPLEASE YOU?

A BRIEF LOOK AT SUICIDAL THOUGHTS

And God saw their works, that they turned from their evil way; and God repented of the evil, that he had said that he would do unto them; and he did it not. **Jonah 3:10**
But it displeased Jonah exceedingly, and he was very angry. 2) And he prayed unto the Lord, and said, I pray thee, O Lord, was not this my saying, when I was yet in my country? Therefore I fled before unto Tarshish: for I knew that thou art a gracious God, and merciful, slow to anger, and of great kindness, and repentest thee of the evil. 3) Therefore now, O Lord, take, I beseech thee, my life from me; for it is better for me to die than to live. 4) Then said the Lord, Doest thou well to be angry?
Jonah 4:1-4

Previously, on our odyssey with Jonah, we found him in the belly of a great fish, at the bottom of the sea, entangled in seaweed. Yet, despite his hopeless situation, despite being completely alone, freezing cold, soaking wet, and totally trapped, Jonah felt a flicker of faith. He mustered an ounce of aspiration as he declared to the Lord …. *I will look again toward thy holy temple* (Jonah 2:4b). He began to encourage himself, as did the Psalmist in the 27th sacred song verses 4-5, who penned, *One thing have I desired of the Lord, that will I seek after; that I may dwell in the house of the Lord all the days of my life, to behold the beauty of the Lord, and to inquire in his temple. For in the time of trouble he shall hide me in his pavilion: in the secret of his tabernacle shall he hide me; he shall set me up upon a rock.*

David and Jonah, in the midst of their respective circumstances, knew that all was not lost. They knew that it was not over for them, and you must know that it is not over for you. Your breakthrough, your deliverance, your healing are nigh. The Lord will hide you. The Lord will guide you. Remember Jonah. The Lord provided a place for him, and he will provide a place for you. David said, *Thou preparest a table before me*

in the presence of mine enemies (Psalm 23:5a).
There is no limit to what God can do. You can
be surrounded by your enemies, and God can
give you a feast. Or you can be facing certain
death, and God can make a way of escape.

Jonah was facing a seemingly impossible
situation; yet, he believed he would worship once
again. He believed he would live to praise the
Lord Most High because his *prayer [had come]*
into [the Lord's] holy temple (Jonah 2:7b) upon
him remembering the Lord. In the words of
David in Psalm 27:13-14, *I had fainted, unless I*
had believed to see the goodness of the Lord in
the land of the living. Wait on the Lord; be of
good courage, and he shall strengthen thine
heart: wait, I say, on the Lord. Your troubles
may seem endless, your situation may appear
dismal, but wait, I say, on the Lord! He is well
able to come through for you.

LYING VANITIES AND FOOLISH BEHAVIOR

As Jonah prayed, he began to reflect on his
foolish behavior, which had landed him in his
perilous plight, and he proclaimed *[They] that*
observe lying vanities forsake their own mercy
(Jonah 2:8).

In other words, "Those who disobey God, in lieu of their own bright ideas, observe lying vanities. Moreover, disobeying God, for whatever reason, is to be led astray by one's own foolish, groundless lies and puts one at risk of not receiving God's amazing grace and wonderful mercy."

Speaking of being led astray by foolish lies, there are those, such as a particular television host and political commentator on HBO, who claim to be atheists. They maintain their disbelief in God's existence with questions like, "How could God allow hurricane Katrina, the BP oil spill, and politicians to behave the way they do?" However, the scriptures plainly state that only *the fool hath said in his heart [there] is no God* (Psalm 14:1). It is this foolish, groundless lie that "there is no God" which has taken prayer out of schools and has allowed sex, violence, and witchcraft to enter in. Additionally, this absurd untruth has enabled state after state to approve gay marriages while a growing number of heterosexual marriages and families have dissolved. Moreover, this ludicrous fallacy has contributed to our nation's all-time high number of teen pregnancies and STDs. Why these evils and a multitude more? The answer is clear: To replace God's divine will with one's own skewed concepts is to remove oneself, with rippling effects on countless others, from God's perfect plan and bountiful blessings.

As we have seen in Jonah's case, one does not have to be a self-proclaimed atheist in order to observe lying vanities or foolish behavior. During my high school years, regretfully, I agreed to a lot of foolish actions, as well. One particular time occurred on a so-called "mischief night" or the night before Halloween. Our church was having a youth program to give the church kids something safe to do, and my sister, her friend, my girlfriend and my girlfriend's sister all decided to walk from my girlfriend's house to the church. On the way to church, we had to pass by a rough section of town. We had walked this way a hundred times before without incident, so we figured it would be okay. However, this time would be different....

I imagine it was all of the Halloween candy, which we had been sneakily eating, that had caused us, this group of usually calm, obedient church kids, to act mischievously. Anyway, my girlfriend came up with the bright idea for us to take a detour *into* the rough section of town and to ring doorbells and run away. I hesitated, warning, "I don't think we should do that." However, the girls were insistent that it would be fun and that nobody would get hurt.

A momentary since of dread came over me. I heard this small voice in the back of my mind saying, "Don't do it, Dennis." But the small voice was outnumbered by those of the girls, so I did not listen. My girlfriend persisted, "It will be fun. After all, it's mischief night." So, despite my better judgment, I went along with the prank.

Like Jonah boarding the cargo ship to sail away from Nineveh, at first things went just fine. The girls would creep up onto someone's porch, ring the doorbell, and then run away and hide. The person whose doorbell they had rung would answer the door and look outside but not see anyone. After looking around for a few minutes and calling out, "Who's there?" the person would return back inside the house. The girls would burst out laughing, imitating the person who had answered the door. Then, they would go past a few houses and do it all again. It seemed like such great fun.

We went about two blocks down the street, then I convinced them to start heading back up the street when, slowly, I began to notice that some of the people were staying on their porches and not going back inside their houses after the girls had rung the doorbells. Even more unsettling to me was a growing group of menacing looking fellows, which had started gathering on the corner in front of us.

Again, similar to Jonah, the girls seemed oblivious to the approaching storm.

I told the girls, "Get ahead of me and speed up." One of the fellows said, "So, you think it's funny to ring people's doorbells, huh?" I could tell from the tension in the air, the look on the man's face, and the tone in his voice that he meant to harm us. So, I told the girls to run. Two of the men took off chasing after them. I managed to trip one and tackle the other, so the girls were able to get away. However, when I looked up, I found myself surrounded by eight or nine men. They all charged me. I managed to take off my belt and use it as a weapon. The belt held them back a little bit, but there were too many of them for me to fight.

Inevitably, two of the men grabbed me from behind while the rest of them started punching and kicking me. The first few punches hurt a lot. But, after that, I stopped feeling the blows. It was strange. It felt as though I were looking down from above, watching myself getting beat up. I think that I was beginning to black out... Suddenly, I heard my sister yell out, "Leave my brother alone! I have a big dog at home, named Duke! I am going to go get him, and he is going to bite all of you!" The men paused, a brief look of concern passed their faces, and then they all burst out laughing.

Meanwhile, a small voice once again spoke to me, telling me, "Run! Run now!" This time, I listened. I was being restrained by two guys; yet, the Lord gave me the strength I needed to break free. I bent down and rose up swinging as hard as I could. I hit the guy in front of me, and he went down. Then, I started to run, stumbling over my belt and almost falling down. I cried out, "O God, please do not let me fall!" And God answered my urgent cry. I managed to catch my balance, and then I took off. They could not catch me! I yelled to the girls to run, and we all escaped. Finally, we all made it to the church safely. Everyone looked at me when we came in, asking "Are you okay? What happened?" I did not realize that I had a busted lip, a black eye, and a knot on my head so big that it looked like I was about to give birth to mini-me.

Yes, I had put myself in danger by being persuaded to act foolishly. Like Jonah who was cast into the sea, I know I should have been killed. However, although I forsook God's mercy, God's mercy did not forsake me. Despite my foolish vanity, God's grace followed me. Just as the fish's belly gave Jonah a place to breathe, my sister's voice gave me a chance to flee. Though I was undeserving, I am so glad that God's grace and mercy preserved me. And I am forever grateful to the Lord, and my sister, for sparing my life.

Truly, as Jonah said in Chapter 2 verse 9b, *Salvation is of the Lord*! I know that someone can relate to what I am saying. Perhaps, you know you should have been dead and gone, but the Lord spared you. The Lord delivered you, even though you did not deserve it. He brought you through, even when you gave him no reason to save you. Praise Jesus for his love that saves us! A songwriter put it this way: "When I think of the goodness of Jesus and all he has done for me, my soul cries out 'Halleluiah! I thank God for saving me!'" And that is precisely why Jesus died on the cross – to save you and me. Jesus, who had never sinned, gave his life to rescue us. Now, by believing in Christ and receiving him as Lord of our lives, we can be free. Yes, truly, salvation is of the Lord.

WHAT IF ... WE HAD A SECOND CHANCE?

And the Lord spake unto the fish, and it vomited out Jonah upon the dry land (Jonah 2:10). Apparently, the fish was a lot smarter than most people because it obeyed God immediately. God told the fish to swallow Jonah, and it did just that without so much as nibbling him. Then, after three days, God instructed the fish to vomit him out, and the fish submitted again by strategically spitting out Jonah onto dry land.

And the word of the Lord came unto Jonah the second time, saying, Arise, go to Nineveh, that great city, and preach unto it the preaching that I bid thee (Jonah 3:1-2). Reminiscent of that voice, which spoke to me for the *second time* on mischief night, we see that God spoke to Jonah for the *second time* regarding his prophetic commission. God, once again, instructed Jonah to go to Nineveh and fulfill his original assignment. He gave Jonah a second chance. See, God's plan and purpose for Jonah never did change. Thus, it was Jonah who had to change. And this time, he did; Jonah obeyed God.

So, Jonah rose up, went to Nineveh, and cried out to its people, warning them that God would destroy their entire city in 40 days. ***So the people of Nineveh believed God*** (Jonah 3:5a). Wow! The people of Nineveh accepted the word of God and from a stranger, at that. That is simply amazing, considering the scriptures give no indication that Jonah performed any miracles or offered the people of Nineveh any counsel or encouragement whatsoever to aid their corporate decision to repent. Jonah only threatened them with God's wrath and ruin.

As a result, the king of Nineveh ordered a city-wide fast. As Jonah 3:7-8 reads, *And he caused it to be proclaimed and published through Nineveh by the decree of the king and his nobles, saying, Let neither man nor beast, herd nor flock, taste any thing: let them not feed, nor drink water: But let man and beast be covered with sackcloth, and cry mightily unto God: Yea, let them turn every one from his evil way, and from the violence that is in their hands.* Thus, the king and his nobles declared an official fast for all living creatures within Nineveh. This makes one wonder, by the ease with which Nineveh received Jonah's message, if, prior to Jonah's arrival, the people of the city had already heard about God's divine intervention concerning Jonah's incredible voyage via the cargo ship sailors.

Can you imagine? A whole city of approximately one million souls agreed to change – to turn from their wicked way, to turn from their violent behavior, to turn from their crude conversation, to turn from their evil actions, and to turn from their sinful intentions. The people of the city agreed to restore what they had unjustly taken by means of force or fraud. Moreover, the people of Nineveh agreed to dress humbly, to abstain from any food or water, and to pray and honor the Most High God.

145

If the people of Nineveh could agree like that, then what on earth would we accomplish if the president, the senate, and congress all agreed on one thing for the benefit of everybody in this country? What kinds of churches would we have, what kinds of families would we raise, and what kinds of marriages would we manifest if everyone agreed to honor God and do what was best for everybody involved? What if we made up our minds never to discourage and always to encourage the positive pursuits of our mates, our children, and the people whom we encounter? What if we decided never to call any of them out of their names, unless we were using terms of endearment, such as "sweetheart", "honey bun", or "handsome"? And what if we chose to put their interests above those of our own?

There is such power in agreement that Jonah 3:10 records, *And God saw their works, that they turned from their evil way; and God repented of the evil, that he had said that he would do unto them; and he did it not.* God heard the remorseful words of the people of Nineveh and saw evidence of their profession through their compunctious actions. That is the essence of genuine repentance: To turn away from or to go in the opposite direction of the wrong way in which one was headed. The people of Nineveh did not offer God blood sacrifices.

Instead, they offered God the sacrifice of broken spirits and contrite hearts, which God did not despise.

WHY ARE YOU DISPLEASED?

But it displeased Jonah exceedingly, and he was very angry (Jonah 4:1). God sparing the city of Nineveh greatly displeased Jonah, and he actually became very angry. Jonah had some nerve. After all, he had been disobedient to God's word; yet, God spared him. He should have fulfilled his assignment, but he tried to escape God's presence; he should have confessed his error, but he was thrown overboard; he should have drowned at sea, but he was swallowed by a great fish; and, he should have been eaten alive, but he was vomited out onto dry land. God had rescued Jonah so that Jonah, in turn, could rescue an entire city. And he did just that. Jonah was successful in completing his God-given mission; and still, he chose to feel exceedingly displeased.

Jonah must not have been thinking rationally because, despite being spared and used by God to spark one of the greatest revivals recorded in Bible history, he felt depressed. The universal repentance and salvation of an entire population actually disappointed him. It seemed as though Jonah had hoped to see Nineveh destroyed.

147

But, how could any sane person even imagine promoting the death of so many people? How could he not rejoice that his message had been hugely successful? I would be ecstatic to lead one soul to salvation, let alone, over one million. Yet, Jonah, behaving in such a self-centered and negative manner, only felt hopelessness and despair, and he begrudged God for having spared the lives of numerous men, women, and children.

How soon did Jonah forget about his heart-wrenching apology to God while trapped in the fish's belly for three long days and three lonely nights? He had pleaded with God to forgive him, but he could not fathom why God forgave all of Nineveh. Thus, in keeping true to the thought pattern of a depressed mind, Jonah took a completely positive situation and turned it into a total negative: "Yes, God spared my life and gave me a second chance. But, that was only to humiliate me. Now, everyone thinks I am a false prophet. I'm a total failure. Things never work out for me. It's all hopeless anyway. I wish I were dead! Why doesn't God just do me a favor and take my life." Depressed people see all roads leading to suicide or death.

In Chapter 4 verse 2, Jonah gave his self-centered explanation for being upset with God. *And he prayed unto the Lord, and said, I pray thee, O Lord, was not this my saying, when I was yet in my country? Therefore I fled before unto Tarshish: for I knew that thou art a gracious God, and merciful, slow to anger, and of great kindness, and repentest thee of the evil.* His concern was never the souls of the city but, rather, himself – *his* reputation, *his* feelings, and how it all affected *him*.

And all he had attributed to God was true: God is gracious, merciful, and kind. Thank God, He is slow to anger, and He is great and greatly to be praised. However, Jonah, in his warped way of thinking, cited these traits to God as though they were something about which He should be ashamed, similarly to when school kids call the "A" students "nerds" or "teachers' pets", or when sexually active teens call virgins "babies" or "stupid", or when alcohol-drinking or drug-using teens call those who abstain "corny" or "uncool". Jonah was essentially doing the same thing; however, he had the foolish audacity to do it to God.

And, as if he had not already said far too much, Jonah then went on to say, *Therefore now, O Lord, take, I beseech thee, my life from me; for it is better for me to die than to live* (Jonah 4:3).

149

Jonah had allowed depression to have such a strong hold on him that he became suicidal in his irrational thinking. He completely discounted God and all His goodness in sparing Nineveh and in sparing him. All he could see was his need for relief and, from his distorted viewpoint, death was the only answer.

In truth, Jonah was in no way ready to die. For, had God taken Jonah up on his offer to let him die after having wished for the death of over a million people, he probably would have gone straight to hell! So God, as loving, patient, merciful, and kind as He is, retorted Jonah's outrageous ranting and request with a question: ***Doest thou well to be angry?*** One Bible translation phrases Jonah 4:4b as thus, "Does doing well displease you?" God responded to Jonah's insanity by asking him, "Do you not like being a success?!"

SAY "YES" TO SUCCESS

God was not harsh in dealing with Jonah. Instead, God used His benevolent treatment of Jonah to provide a perfect example of how we may help to restore one who has slid down an emotion spiral of guilt, regret, depression, and anger to thoughts of suffering and suicide. He demonstrated how, through His love, we can ease one's emotional anguish by helping that person call to mind past personal successes and victories. As Proverbs 15:1a reminds us, *[a] soft answer turneth away wrath.*

The person needing comfort may insist, "Nothing good ever happens to me. Nothing ever works out the way I want." And, we could agree with the truth: "Yes, it is true that everything does not always work out exactly as you want it to. You are right; everything is not perfect. I know people have hurt you; I know you feel pain. And I know you have lost some things. But, you are not alone because Jesus said that he would never leave nor forsake you. All is not lost, and nothing is over until God says it is over. God has the final say and, as long as the sun rises in the east and sets in the west, tomorrow is another day. So, there is still hope."

And there is hope for you, too. Remember, God delivered Daniel out of the lions' den, so He can certainly deliver you from the depths of depression. Even if you, like Joseph, have been beaten, betrayed, and thrown in the pit by your own family and friends, God can raise you up again. Who knows? He may place you in a position to help them. So, be encouraged, and don't give up. Do not give up hope because it's never too late. Though things may look bad now, joy does come in the morning. So, listen to me: Get up out of bed. Brush your teeth. Wash your face. Shower, put your clothes on, and put a smile on your face. For, this day, which you have lived to see, is the day that the Lord has made. Rejoice, and be glad and grateful to see it.

True, you may be experiencing depressed or bad feelings. But, you are not those feelings. You are not those experiences. What you have been feeling can change, and what you have been experiencing can change. Despite all of the crazy things you have been through, *you do have value.* God has a plan for you; there is something He wants you to do. Don't be like Jonah and discount all the wonderful things that God has done for you. And do not let the history or the hope of doing well displease you. It is evident that God has done something good for you because you are alive today. You ate something. You slept somewhere. You have clothes on your back, and you have this book in your hand. (Even if you could not afford to buy it and someone gave it to you, you still were blessed with it.) And because God has blessed you before, you can rest assured that He will bless you again. Say "yes" to success for your life by saying "yes" to God's love and will for your life.

CHAPTER 7

IS BEING ANGRY WORKING FOR YOU?

SURVEYING THE EMOTION OF ANGER

Then said the Lord, Doest thou well to be angry? 5) So Jonah went out of the city, and sat on the east side of the city, and there made him a booth, and sat under it in the shadow, till he might see what would become of the city. 6) And the Lord God prepared a gourd, and made it to come up over Jonah, that it might be a shadow over his head, to deliver him from his grief. So Jonah was exceeding glad of the gourd. **Jonah 4:4-6**

In this portion of our text, we find the Lord questioning Jonah's great displeasure regarding His sovereign decision to spare the inhabitants of Nineveh upon their repentance in response to Jonah's warning. Obviously, he quickly forgot that God, with Whom he was so displeased, was the same merciful and gracious One Who had recently spared him

153

from a series of unimaginable events – being caught in a tempest aboard a cargo ship; being tossed overboard into a stormy sea; being swallowed whole by a great fish; being trapped in the fish's belly for three days; and, being vomited out of the fish's mouth onto dry land.

Yes, the people of Nineveh had been sinful, and they deserved God's judgment in recompense for their iniquitous ways. However, Jonah also had been in error. A prophet of God and a descendant of His chosen people, Jonah should have known better than anyone not to disobey Him. Yet, he sinned against God by ignoring His divine command to preach to Nineveh. Not only did Jonah disappoint God with his own sin, but he had the unmitigated gall to be disappointed with God for forgiving the sins of numerous others.

BARGAINING WITH GOD

Seemingly, as soon as Jonah had been delivered from his self-inflicted ordeal at sea, selective amnesia set in and he dismissed God's kind dealings with him in hopes of witnessing God deal harshly with the people of Nineveh. How sad that Jonah chose to be so judgmental regarding the plight of others? How unfortunate that he seemingly wished to see others suffer for their transgressions?

At one time or another, everyone needs God's deliverance and forgiveness. At one time or another, everyone faces a situation so serious that only the Lord Himself could see him or her through. In fact, if we were truthful, many of us would admit to having been in a predicament so precarious that we actually pleaded God's divine favor in exchange for some sort of future sacrifice, obedience, or allegiance on our part. For me, that time occurred shortly after I had graduated from dental school...

For my second job after graduation, I worked at a dental clinic. Most of the patients there were single moms and their kids. One day, I happened to mention to the receptionist who worked with me that I thought one of my patients was very pretty. Unbeknownst to me, the receptionist mistook my comment about my patient's looks as a subtle request for her to set the two of us up on a date, which she did. So, I agreed to take my patient out, we had a good time, and we even started dating.

(BUT, HERE'S A FRIENDLY WARNING TO ANY PROFESSIONAL: *Never date or become romantically involved with any of your patients or your staff because, unless you marry the person, no matter how great it may seem initially, things will always end badly ... ALWAYS.*)

Anyway, my patient had a 6 or 7 year old child. Thus, I was a little concerned she might still be involved with her child's father. So, I asked her about him, and she assured me that she had not seen him in over four years. She also told me that he never came around to see them and that he did not even pay child support. She added that she had no idea where he was or what he had been doing. So, I decided it would be okay for us to continue dating.

One afternoon, while we were at my patient's apartment, her child fell asleep. We saw it as a golden opportunity to fool around. So, we went into her bedroom, closed and locked the door, and proceeded to become intimate. Suddenly, we heard someone knocking loudly on her front door. Bang, bang, bang! A Latin male voice shouted, "Let me in! Let me in!" Naturally, the child, who had been sound asleep, woke up from the noise of, what turned out to be, the father yelling and pounding on the front door. Startled by the commotion, we stopped what we were doing and lie frozen as we listened to the father convince the child to open the front door! We untangled ourselves and went into a full panic!

I feared that her screaming mad ex-husband was going to see us together and kill us. So, I began to pray: "Oh, Lord, *please,* HELP ME. I do not want to get shot or stabbed. Please, Lord, if you get me out of this, I promise I will stop fooling around with my patients. *I promise!*" I did not know what to do, so I began questioning her: "I thought you said your ex-husband never comes around?!" She answered, "He doesn't." To that, I replied, "Well, he sure is here *now!*"

She told me to get dressed. Then, her ex started banging on the bedroom door, demanding that she let him in so the two of them could "talk". She reasoned with him through the bedroom door: "Calm down. Why are you acting like this? It's over. Leave me alone, so I can make a new life for me and our child." All the while she was stalling him through the closed door I was fumbling with my clothes. But, I was so nervous that I just could not seem to get them on. Thankfully, I managed to put on my underwear and socks, but her enraged ex-husband was still pounding on the bedroom door, threatening to kill both of us.

The door seemed moments away from flinging open. And, though I could have stood there and fought, the truth is I had been caught totally off guard. (I was frightened and still too worn out from fooling around.) Thus, I decided it would be best for me to run away, so I would live to fight another day. Her ex had been pounding on the door so forcefully that I thought it would burst open at any second. So, I grabbed the rest of my clothes and threw them out of the window. (She lived on the second floor of the apartment building.) Just as the bedroom door flew open, I jumped out the window. Landing safely, I grabbed my clothes and shoes and took off running. Her ex-husband yelled at me through the window but, thankfully, he did not jump out to chase after me.

I made it to my car, where I finished getting dressed. After taking a moment to collect myself, (it had been quite an ordeal), I decided I should call her to make sure that she was okay. She assured me she was fine and she had called the police, so he left. I then returned to her apartment so we could talk. However, after such a harrowing experience, for me, the thrill of our relationship was gone. Not long after that we broke up, but I certainly was not going to forget the promise I had made to God when I was in the midst of trouble – "God, if you get me out of this safely, I will not get involved with my patients anymore." Thank God, He got me out safely and, in return, I have kept my word.

Now, hopefully, you never had to jump out of a second story window like I did, and you never had to be vomited out of a fish's mouth like our friend Jonah. But, I do believe that most people, including you, have faced circumstances that have gotten so far out of control that they started bargaining with God. I know you have heard it said, or maybe, you have said it: "Lord, if "You' just send me the money I need, I promise to pay my tithes and give a generous offering." "Lord, if "You" save my marriage and family, I promise to be faithful to my spouse and spend more time with my kids." "Lord, if "You" let me pass this test, I promise to study every day." "Lord, if "You" keep me from getting caught, I promise not to drink or get high ever again." "Lord, heal me, and I'll…" "Lord, heal my baby, and I'll…" "Lord, help my children and I'll…" "Do not let the boss see me or fire me, Lord, and I'll…" "Lord, I am lonely. Let me get married, and I'll…" "Please, God, I will serve "You". God, I will do whatever "You" want me to do if only You will deliver me."

Thank God He is longsuffering toward us, not willing that any of us should perish. He hears the petitions of His people in trouble just like He heard my desperate cry in my patient's bedroom and like He heard Jonah's urgent prayer in the fish's belly. Because of God's faithfulness toward us, we can agree with the song writer, who penned: *I was sinking deep in sin, far from the peaceful shore… …sinking to rise no more. But the Master of the sea, heard my despairing cry, from the waters lifted me, now safe am I. [God's] love lifted me* (lyrics by James Rowe). I am so grateful that God's love does lift us. Once we dedicate our lives to Him, we become His dear children. And we are never so alone, never so lost, never so wrong, and never so far away that He cannot make a way for us out of no way.

CRAZY … BUT CONVINCING

Truly, God did provide a way out for Jonah, for after three days … ***the Lord [spoke] unto the fish, and it vomited out Jonah upon the dry land*** (Jonah 2:10). ***And the word of the Lord came unto Jonah the second time, saying, Arise, go unto Nineveh, that great city, and preach unto it the preaching that I bid thee. So Jonah arose, and went unto Nineveh, according to the word of the Lord. Now Nineveh was an exceeding great city of three day's journey. And Jonah began to enter into the city a day's journey, and he cried, and said, Yet forty days, and Nineveh shall be overthrown. So the people of Nineveh believed God,*** (Jonah 3:1-5a).

Isn't that amazing?! The king, his nobles, and the people of Nineveh believed what Jonah told them. I find this truly incredible considering how he must have appeared to them. I imagine that Jonah was smelly, looked raggedy, and acted completely crazy. In other words, Jonah was a hot mess!

Remember that Jonah was *vomited* up onto shore, and if fish vomit smells anything like dog or human vomit, it is putrid. Moreover, Jonah had been in the fish's belly for *three days*, so where did he go to the bathroom? Unless the fish came equipped with a port-a-potty, Jonah must have relieved himself on himself or somewhere inside the fish. Once on dry land, Jonah then had to walk to Nineveh (a city that was three day's journey in size), where he travelled inland about *a day's journey*. Undoubtedly, he was exhausted, sweaty, and smelly. Whew! Jonah was rank!

Let us not forget what Jonah must have looked like. He had been below deck on a cargo ship; flung about with a bunch of sailors in a violent storm; and, hurled into the ocean, only to be swallowed by a gigantic fish. If airlines commonly lose luggage when passengers connect flights, is it highly unlikely that whatever wardrobe Jonah had been carrying kept up with him throughout his various, unscheduled modes of transportation? And, unless his money made it with him overboard into the fish, through the seaweed, past the vomit, and onto dry land, I think it is safe to say that he was unable to purchase any new clothing at Nineveh's nearest mall. Thus, Jonah was forced to preach his sermon in clothes that were wet, tattered, and torn.

And how must Jonah have acted? Put it this way: How would you have acted if you had been caught at sea in a life-threatening storm; thrown overboard by a band of sailors; swallowed whole by an enormous fish; trapped inside its belly with no food, water, facilities, sunlight, or human contact for three days; sent flying through the air from its mouth onto the ground; and, then, have to walk for an entire day – all to deliver a sermon to a congregation, which you were reluctant to face in the first place?! And all the while you were experiencing all this mayhem you knew that it was your disobedience to God, which had landed you in such dire straits, so all of it was your own fault!! To say that Jonah was acting crazy probably is a gross understatement.

Thus, Jonah smelled, looked, and acted like a total nut case. Yet, the people of Nineveh, even its royalty, believed him. John the Baptist came across as a wild man. He lived in the woods and was unkempt in his appearance. Still, he preached the baptism of repentance so effectively that the surrounding city residents believed him. Even Jesus Christ was baptized by him. Apostle Paul was frail and half blind. However, he established a multitude of churches in numerous countries, and his letters constitute most of the New Testament of the Bible.

I am persuaded that it does not matter what you look like or how you dress. Your clothes, house, and car are unimportant to God. Your heart and His word are what matters to Him. *For the word of God is quick, and powerful, and sharper than any [two-edged] sword, piercing, even to the dividing asunder of soul and spirit, and of the joints and marrow, and is a discerner of the thoughts and intents of the heart* (Hebrew 4:12). God's word does not need your house, car, or clothes. It can do without your titles, degrees, or pedigree. His word stands on its own merit, and God chooses the vessels He desires to deliver His word.

The one who delivers God's word is like the pump, which delivers gas to a car. No one pays much attention to the gas pump. What one cares about is the gas because it is the gas which fuels the car. It is God's word which fuels and feed are spirits, souls, and lives. Thus, if a messenger of God's word becomes too full of himself (or herself), he can easily be replaced.

God can use a donkey to deliver His word. The rocks can cry out the praises of God. The birds, trees, mountains, seas, and all of nature testify of God's worth. I like to think that I am smarter than a rock or donkey, although that might be debatable. However, I do know enough not to want any rocks crying out for me. Therefore, I will praise Him. I will glorify and magnify the Lord. And, as long as the Lord desires me to do so, I will deliver His word. In the words of Prophet Isaiah, *Here am I; send me* (Isaiah 6:8b). That is how God wants us to present ourselves to Him: with a humble and willing spirit, saying, "Here I am, Lord. Send me."

ANGER HAPPENS

So the people of Nineveh believed God, and proclaimed a fast, and put on sackcloth, from the greatest of them even to the least of them. [And the king said,] Who can tell if God will turn and repent, and turn away from his fierce anger, that we perish not? And God saw their works, that they turned from their evil way: and God repented of the evil, that he had said that he would do unto them; and he did it not. But it displeased Jonah exceedingly, and he was very angry. Then said the Lord, Doest thou well to be angry? (Jonah 3:5, 9-10; 4:1, 4).

Now, many people would claim that they *never* get angry, that they are *always* in control of their emotions. However, the increasing consumption of prescription blood pressure and anti-depressant medications among Americans today would indicate otherwise. In truth, most of us get angry at times and for various reasons.

Some people experience anger when driving in their cars. Another driver may dart out in front of them or change lanes without signaling or drive like molasses in front of them, refusing to get out of the way. I find it especially annoying when a driver tailgates me so closely that it looks like the bumper of his car is going to come through my rear view mirror. My sister is one of those drivers who will not give way for another driver to edge into traffic. For example, when a driver is exiting the gas station and signals to ask her to let him into the lane, my Holy Ghost-filled, fire-baptized, I-got-Jesus-on-my-side sister will turn up her nose, look away, and inch up to close the gap between her and the car in front of her!

Also, I used to have a secretary who actually made a practice of stealing parking spaces! She would observe as a driver would back out of a parking space at Wal-Mart, Smith's or some other store, and another driver would patiently await that space, blinking signal light and all. Then, with her compact car, she would approach from the other side and zip right into the parking space. She then would hop out of her car and go into the store, ignoring the other driver … who, of course, would curse her out. Yes, anger happens among drivers.

Not only do drivers become angry with other drivers, but parents sometimes become angry with their own children, and over the simplest things. For example, parents might get irritated by their children whining for dessert, like cookies and ice cream, knowing that at mealtime they barely touched their plates. And how irksome is it for the parents whose baby sleeps soundly through an entire church worship service but, at 3:00 in the morning when all is quiet and they want to get some much needed rest, the little darling is wide awake and crying? Yes, anger happens in parenting.

What is truly amazing is how people's loved ones often anger them more than anyone else. Overtime, "honey bun", "baby doll", and "sweetheart" can turn into "stupid", "imbecile", or "jerk". Boy, oh boy! Can spouses provoke anger? Often, a spouse may say one thing but seem to do another. For example, a wife may ask her husband, "Do you enjoy being with me?" Naturally, he says, "Yes." But his attitude or actions may indicate the contrary because he would rather watch "the game" on television or work outside on his truck than spend ten minutes alone in conversation with his wife.

Some wives complain, "My husband just doesn't seem into me, and he never shows me affection in public." So, not surprisingly, when their husbands approach them at night, they pull away and respond, "Not tonight; I'm just not in the mood." Also, husbands commonly complain that their wives give them the silent treatment. "I know something is bugging you," they might suggest to their better halves. Yet, rather than talk, their wives may opt to have attitudes. On the other hand, when wives insist to their husbands, "Let's talk about it" (whatever "it" might be), and their husbands change the subjects, they often will assume to know what their husbands were thinking or would say. If the husbands then insist, "That is not what I was going to say," many times, the wives refuse to believe them, accusing them of covering up their true feelings.

Sadly, married people frequently treat total strangers better than they do their own mates. Think about it: If someone bumps into a woman at the mall or steps on her big toe, she probably would not give it a second thought and would be quick to accept the person's apology: "That's okay. No problem. I know it was an accident." But, let her own husband bump into her or step on her big toe. She likely would be furious: "You did that on purpose. You say, 'There are no accidents,' so I know you meant to do it. You're just getting back at me for something!"

Moreover, jealousy between spouses can easily produce anger. If a husband (or wife) is being faithful and his wife accuses him of infidelity, they both can become angry. She is mad because she can't catch him or prove it, though she feels sure of her suspicion; and, he is ticked off because he is in trouble with his wife, though he knows he has done nothing wrong! And, oh boy, do not be the husband who is guilty of being unfaithful and gets caught by the wife... "I knew it! I knew you were cheating on me! You must think I'm stupid!" Yes, anger most definitely happens in marriage.

I feel certain that we all have faced anger. Whether from the pressures of work, family, finances, school, church, relationships, social

168

standing, or otherwise, we all, at least once, have been angry, heated, perturbed, provoked, annoyed, irked, irritated, vexed, or just plain ticked off. And the anger we face is not always initially evident. Sometimes it gradually creeps up on us like a slow, steady burn until we become … *burning mad*! But, however unintentional our anger might be, anger does happen. And it happens to us all.

DO YOU MEAN "YOU CAN'T" … OR "YOU *WON'T*"?

Anger certainly happened to Jonah, the prophet of God. As a matter of fact in Chapter 4 verse 1 of our text, we see that Jonah was *displeased exceedingly* and *very angry*. **Then said the Lord, Doest thou well to be angry?** The Lord Most High asked His prophet, Jonah, a question. But Jonah did not answer. Instead, *[he] went out of the city, and sat on the east side of the city, and there made him a booth, and sat under it in the shadow, till he might see what would become of the city.*

Jonah wanted to have a good view of the city in order to see what would become of it. Would God destroy the city or spare it? Jonah likely had expected that if God would not demolish the city, He would at least inflict on it some horrible secondary judgment, like a plague that would kill half of its population. Jonah was hoping for some sort of catastrophe to happen to Nineveh to keep him from looking bad or like a false prophet. So, Jonah left the city and positioned himself so as to witness what he felt was the well-deserved wrath of God upon its inhabitants.

But, what if Jonah had stayed? Considering the readiness with which Nineveh received Jonah and his message from God, surely they would have wanted him to stay and perhaps counsel them regarding repentance and righteousness. Certainly the king of Nineveh would have shown him respect, honor, and great gratitude for alerting them to the error of their ways and the judgment of God, which was to befall them. It is possible that the king would have gone so far as to shower Jonah with possessions, sustenance, and female company; declare him an honorary prince; and, gift him with a key to the city. If only he had stayed beyond delivering his warning to the people in order to prepare or instruct them on how to make amends with God, undoubtedly, the king would have shown Jonah some form of appreciation.

Nonetheless, if there had been a royal invitation for Jonah to remain in the city of Nineveh, he evidently refused it. Jonah declined the king's gracious hospitality, as I imagine it, with some sort of excuse: "I would stay, but I don't want to be caught in the coming destruction." "I want to stay, but my cat died." "I'd like to stay, but my big toe hurts. My arthritis flares up when a storm is coming." "Thanks anyway for the invitation, but the kids have school in the morning." Jonah probably found some lame reason to bow out gracefully, just as most of us do when we feel reluctant to do something or go somewhere. We create excuses and hope the other party is sharp enough or polite enough not to question or challenge the excuses we invent.

Apparently, the king and citizens of Nineveh did just that. Whatever explanation Jonah had offered, I am sure they knew was a fabrication. And they undoubtedly felt rejected by Jonah. But, what could they have done? "Perhaps," they may have convinced themselves, "he has another city to save, and he must get to it right away." No one, no matter who it may be, likes to feel rejected.

Speaking of rejection, Jonah's actions toward the people of Nineveh brings to mind parents, guardians, foster parents, and adoptive parents who have or take in children, then act like they really do not want, love, or value them. Parental rejection only serves to confuse, frustrate, or anger children and create feelings of hostility, bitterness, and a little craziness. After all, why should people take in or produce children and then ignore, neglect, mistreat, or abuse them? I know such behavior from a parent would make me angry, crazy, or both.

So, what if the children are not perfect? Here's a news flash: Neither am I nor you. However, I Corinthians 1:27-28 reminds us *...God hath chosen the foolish things of the world* - the odd, the overweight, the awkwardly tall, the unattractive – *to confound [or to confuse] the wise; and God hath chosen the weak things of the world* – the frail, the tiny, the skinny – *to confound [or confuse] the things which are mighty; And base things of the world, and things which are despised,* – the poor, the rejected, the unaccepted of any race or color – *hath God chosen, yea, and things which are not, to bring to nought [to nothing] things that are...*

Yes, you may feel as though you are on the bottom now; you may feel rejected now. But *...it is written, Eye hath not see, nor ear heard, neither have entered into the heart of man, the things which God hath prepared for them that love him* (I Corinthians 2:9). And like the *stone which the builder rejected, the same is become the head of the corner: this is the Lord's doing,* *and it is marvelous in our eyes…* (Matthew 21:42b). Truly, it is wondrous and glorious what the Lord will do for us.

SO, YOU'RE ANGRY? HOW'S THAT WORKING FOR YOU?

So Jonah went out of the city, and sat on the east side of the city, and there made him a booth, and sat under it in the shadow, till he might see what would become of the city (Jonah 4:5). Isn't it funny how angry people, in the heat of their emotions, often do things that make little or no sense.

Sometimes, angry people destroy their own property. They may break dishes, glasses, or picture frames. Some smash television sets or punch holes in walls. Others kick down doors, breaking a toe or foot. Then, once they have calmed themselves down, they have to buy new dishes or a new television, replace the door, or see a doctor, with embarrassment I am sure, about their self-inflicted injury.

Certain people become so enraged at loved ones that they throw away objects of sentimental value, such as wedding or engagement rings, family heirlooms, or photo albums. Others put themselves in harm's way by storming out of the safety of an apartment or house in the middle of the night just to sleep in a parked car or on a park bench. There are those who become so furious with mechanics, plumbers, or other craftsmen (or women) that they attempt to do the ridiculous. For instance, someone who has never before changed a tire on a car, because of anger, will set out to change an entire transmission or install a new muffler. Or, one who knows absolutely nothing about water pipes, due to upset feelings, will take on the project of remodeling an entire bathroom, vowing to have it done in a day.

Seemingly, angry people purposefully go out of their way to inconvenience themselves, perhaps on some subconscious level, so as to create new problems about which to complain. A girlfriend yells at her beau, "Let me out! I do not need you or your stupid car! I will walk home." "Oh, come on. It's 12:00 midnight, and you live fifteen miles away," he reasons with her. "Humph! Like you care?" she retorts as she reaches for the door handle. Meanwhile, she is wearing an evening gown and five-inch heels, which have been hurting her feet all evening. And as she climbs out of the car, she tears her dress, but she continues to storm down the street away from her boyfriend's car. She then breaks her heel, but she keeps on hobbling away. Suddenly, it starts to rain. Now, she is angry at you, the car, her dress, her shoes, the rain, and her sore feet, not to mention her bruised ego.

Sounds similar to what Jonah did, right? He could have stayed in the king's palace or in Nineveh's most luxurious hotel (or something of the sort). Instead, Jonah stormed off to sit in a *booth*, which he had made out of tree branches and leaves. What a tough decision that would have been for someone else? "Hmmm, let's see… should I stay in the king's royal palace or at a lavish hotel, or should I stay in a flimsy, hastily-made leaf booth. Hmmm, king's palace versus leaf booth – that's a tough one."

Now, to tell the truth, I would have done like Nineveh and let Jonah storm off mad. Sure, I would have. I would have said, "Well, go on then. Leave. See if I care!" Oh, admit it, in the heat of an argument, you do not always behave patiently and with kindness. I know I am not the only one who has ever misbehaved or said something unkind in anger. Like me, if you have ever loved somebody, then you have gotten angry, on some level, with that somebody. And when you became angry, it is possible that you behaved a little like Jonah.

And the Lord God prepared a gourd, and made it to come up over Jonah, that it might be a shadow over his head, to deliver him from his grief. So Jonah was exceeding glad of the gourd (Jonah 4:6). Thankfully, God is so patient, loving, and kind that he prepared a large leafy plant for Jonah because He knew his make-shift booth would have been insufficient to protect him from the elements. God did not allow Jonah just to go storming off steaming mad. But, as the Good Shepherd Who cares and searches for His lost sheep, He made provision for Jonah. Although Jonah, in his anger, acted childishly and impulsively, God used the gourd to protect him from freezing in the extreme cold at night and from baking in the blazing sun during the day.

Isn't God awesome? He makes provision for us. Despite how foolishly we may behave, despite all we may do or what may be done to us, His love yet provides for us. His grace and mercy simply will not leave us alone. Yes, we do get angry. But, as God questioned in Jonah 4:4, *Doest [us] well to be angry*? In other words, "Is being angry working for us? Is anger working in our favor?" It is okay to be angry, but what do we do with the anger? The Bible tells us in Ephesians 4:26a, *Be ye angry, and sin not...* Thus, when we become angry, we must not make things worse with our own poor reactions.

When things come to upset us, we must remember, "I am not the only one facing problems or challenges." Above all, rest assured that come whatever problems, the Lord Almighty is able to solve them. Joseph was thrown into a pit and left for dead, but the Lord raised him up instead. Daniel was thrown into the lions' den, but the Lord delivered him. The Hebrew lads were thrown into a fiery oven, but the Lord's angel came to join them. Just as God rescued them back then, He still is able to rescue any one of us today.

CHAPTER 8

GOD'S REMEDY FOR ANGER

TRAVERSING THE EMOTIONS OF ANGER AND GRIEF

And the Lord God prepared a gourd, and made it to come up over Jonah, that it might be a shadow over his head, to deliver him from his grief. So Jonah was exceeding glad of the gourd. 7) But God prepared a worm when the morning rose the next day, and it smote the gourd that it withered. 8) And it came to pass, when the sun did arise, that God prepared a vehement east wind; and the sun beat upon the head of Jonah, that he fainted, and wished in himself to die, and said, It is better for me to die than to live. 9) And God said to Jonah, Doest thou well to be angry for the gourd? And he said, I do well to be angry, even unto death. 10) Then said the Lord, Thou hast had pity on the gourd, for the which thou hast not labored, neither madest it grow; which came up in a night, and perished in a night: 11) And should not I spare Nineveh, that great city, wherein are more than sixscore thousand persons that

cannot discern between their right hand and their left hand; and also much cattle?
Jonah 4:6-11

At this point in Jonah's expedition, we observe that the Lord, in His loving kindness, prepared a large, leafy plant to shield Jonah from the harsh desert elements after he had hastily departed the city of Nineveh. What a patient and benevolent Father our God is to make provision for Jonah considering the impetuous and juvenile manner in which he had behaved? Jonah actually was displeased with God for deciding to spare the citizen's of Nineveh from their forthcoming judgment after they had repented and initiated a corporate fast. *So Jonah went out of the city, and sat on the east side of the city, and there made him a booth, and sat under it in the shadow, till he might see what would become of the city*

Wow! Jonah had the nerve to argue with God because the events in Nineveh did not transpire as he had hoped; and, then, he had the audacity to storm off. If it were me, I would have been afraid to say anything to God but, "Yes, Lord." After all, if God could create a storm that almost broke a ship in two and if God even considered destroying a city, what could He have done to me? Nineveh, a city of over a million people, repented and God pardoned them, which was cause for celebration. Instead, Jonah was filled with frustration. He obviously was not thinking straight because he actually caught an attitude with God.

But God, Who is so loving and longsuffering toward us, *prepared a gourd, and made it to come up over Jonah, that it might be a shadow over his head, to deliver him from his grief* (Jonah 4:6a). It is interesting that the scripture notes, "God made a gourd to be a shadow over Jonah's head *to deliver him from his GRIEF*?"

THERE'S NOTHING GOOD ABOUT GRIEF, CHARLIE BROWN

Grief is described as emotional suffering caused by a loss. Typically, we think of grief as associated with the death or loss of a loved one, such as a spouse, child, or parent. However, the loss of a dream, vision, or life goal can also trigger feelings of grief.

My life goal upon entering dental school was to become an oral surgeon. Unfortunately, I was not accepted to a post-graduate oral surgery program. Later, after I had been in private practice for about four years, I dreamed of becoming the Mc Donald's of general dentistry. I envisioned having a dental franchise with offices in four or more locations. I branched out as far as obtaining a second dental office. Sadly, with two offices and two staffs, all I did was double my bills.

Moreover, in the two and a half years I had two offices I must have hired and fired ten different dentists. The problem was the only dentist that would work hard for me was me. On any given day, whichever office I would work in would generate money. However, whichever office my dental associate would cover for the day would produce no money. I went so far as to make surprise visits to the unsupervised office, and, of course, the staff and associate dentist all would act busy. But, as soon as I had left, all work would come to a screeching halt. It was as if they would say, "Hey, the boss is gone. Let's order pizza and beer and have a party."

And I had my share of characters working for me as associate dentists. One of them, I later was informed by a nearby oral surgeon, made it his business to refer all potential tooth extractions out to his oral surgery office.

Another associate was seen by a staff member shooting up drugs outside in the parking lot. Then, there was this female associate dentist who would constantly have "a problem" or "an emergency" for which she would call me to come right over to her aid. However, not much time passed before she revealed her true motives for the frequent calls – she fantasized of marrying me! Lastly, one associate told me right to my face that no other dentist was ever going to work hard for me. After that conversation, I admitted to myself that he was right, and I let the second office go. But it hurt to think of all the time, money, and effort I had wasted. So, I grieved over the loss of my dream.

I also have had to grieve over the loss of a marriage. As previously mentioned in **Chapter 5: God Will Remember You,** I was once married before. It seemed as though the marriage was doomed from the start because we never got along. Actually, I married her during the time I had opened and was trying to operate the second dental office. Therefore, I would like to think if I did not have the stress of two offices, I would have behaved better in our marriage. In truth, however, I most likely would have behaved just as badly. I cheated on her a lot. Looking back, I suppose I married her because I thought getting married would have made my life easier, but it did not. Our marriage only lasted about two years. Thankfully we did not have any kids as a result of our union.

Still, much to my surprise, even the end of the bad marriage hurt. It left me feeling like a failure, like I was incapable of being loved. I actually remember wondering if I would ever again be able to love or to be loved. Thus, whether the loss is that of a loved one, a marriage or relationship, or a hope or dream, it hurts. And I believe we all have experienced loss. We all have known grief.

The question is, "What had Jonah lost besides his temper?" Did Jonah in some way feel he had lost status as a prophet by being the first whom God had sent to preach to the Gentiles rather than to his kinsmen in Israel? Or, did Jonah imagine a loss of status for the children of Israel as the chosen people of God because He had chosen to spare them from divine judgment?

Could it be that Jonah thought God should only care for and protect the children of Israel, similar to when an only child suddenly has to welcome a new baby brother or sister into the

183

family? The child then must face the reality of having to share the parents' attention and affection with a cute, little, crying, pooping, demanding competitor. Some children adjust to this change quickly and calmly, while others resist and act out in order to be noticed. Still, other children become angry and seek to remove or rid of the little intruder.

Unfortunately, many adults tend to behave a lot like children, not handling loss or grief in a quiet, calm, or dignified manner. Many people get angry, blaming everyone else for their unhappy situations. They say, "It's the doctor's fault." "It's the hospital's fault." "It's the insurance company's fault." "It's my parents' fault." "It's my husband's fault." "It's the school's fault, the cat's fault, or the dog's fault this happened to me." "I am angry, and somebody is to blame. Somebody has to pay." Either we have said these things, or we know someone who has said these things.

REJOICE IN THE LORD, NOT IN THE GOURD

But, what is the answer to grief? What seems to be the cure? In verse 6 of our text, we see that God prepared a gourd to give Jonah shade and to deliver him from his grief. Think about it: When we feel better physically, we tend to feel better mentally, emotionally, and spiritually. A back rub does wonders for me.

Section "b" of verse 6 goes on to say, ***So Jonah was exceeding glad of the gourd.*** Jonah was elated and overjoyed because of the large, leafy plant. See, instead of thanking God for the gourd, which sprung up so quickly to cover his head, he viewed it as some sort of justification for his actions. You know how we act when we insist we are right: "Oh Yeah! I knew I was right. You see? I am winning this argument. My football [or basketball] team won, which proves I am a winner and you are a l-o-o-o-o-s-e-r. Next time, you will listen to me." Jonah felt the same way – like he was winning the argument with God or that he was justified in his anger toward God for not destroying the city of Nineveh.

But God prepared a worm when the morning rose the next day, and it [attacked] the gourd that it [shriveled up] (Jonah 4:7). God basically was saying, "No, Jonah, I only wanted to shelter you and relieve you of your grief. I did not prepare the gourd to justify your bad behavior and mean thinking." Thus, God took the gourd away.

Jonah was joyful over the gourd, and God allowed it to be attacked and to wither away. This just goes to show how fleeting and fragile are material things. Sure, we are happy if we buy a new house or car. But, the truth is most of us are four missed pay checks away from bankruptcy. Some of us are only two missed pay checks away from financial ruin. Thus, is it safe for us to receive our exceeding great joy from our houses, clothing, cars, or other material possessions?

It is true that Jesus said, *I am come that [you] might have life, and that you [you] might have it more abundantly* (John 10:10b), so God does want us to be blessed and to enjoy nice things. In fact, when we accept Christ into our lives we are adopted into God's royal family. We become joint-heirs to the throne and children of the Most High. And, as such, God wants us to have the best of everything because the cattle on a thousand hills belong to Him, and we belong to Him, too.

At the same time, as Apostle Paul exhorted in Philippians 3:1 and 4:4, we should *...rejoice in the Lord.* Let us reserve our exceeding great joy for the One Who gives us the resources, power, ability, and favor to acquire houses, cars, promotions, etc. All of life's comforts – the house, the car, the widescreen television, the iPad, the computer – are just gourds. They have their roots in the earth, in materiality, and our grasp on them is delicate. However, something subtle, like a worm, a layoff, a divorce, an illness, tax problems, even a bad decision, can cause our gourds, or life's comforts, to wither away.

Even if your gourd, your life's comforts, does not vanish from you completely, it can shrivel up to the point that it is of no use to you. A small, insignificant worm can cause your house or car to lose all of the pleasure it once gave you. Perhaps, the house will have plumbing problems or its roof will leak. Or maybe, your nice car will stay in the repair shop or end up being repossessed. Those comforts were just gourds.

What we should remember, instead, is to trust in the Lord, to hold on to the Rock of Ages. We must not fall, as did Jonah, into the trap of rejoicing and trusting in the gourd. Affirm with me these words coined by Edward Mote: *My hope is built on nothing less than Jesus' blood and righteousness. I dare not trust the sweetest frame, but wholly [lean] on Jesus' name. On Christ the solid rock I stand, all other ground is sinking sand; all other ground is sinking sand.*

And it came to pass, when the sun did arise, that God prepared a vehement east wind; and the sun beat upon the head of Jonah, that he fainted, and wished in himself to die, and said, It is better for me to die than to live (Jonah 4:8). Up to this point, God had prepared four different things for Jonah's good: 1. a great fish to save him; 2. a gourd to comfort him; 3. a worm to correct him; and now, 4. a powerful wind to teach him a lesson. Once again, we are reminded through God's gracious dealings with Jonah that *...all things work together for good to them that love God, to them who are the called according to his purpose* (Romans 8:28).

Take note of Jonah still behaving and thinking irrationally. Clearly, he was still experiencing grief and anger, as the statement he made – *It is better for me to die than to live* – placed so little value on his life. To think, Jonah figured, since the weed had died, he should die also. In his illogical thoughts, Jonah saw his own life as equivalent to and connected to the life of a weed. It seems foolish of Jonah, but we do the same thing when we think our value is tied or bound to our material possessions.

Regrettably, too many of us think if we lose our house or our car, then we are nothing and our lives are worth nothing. However, this kind of thinking is dangerously incorrect. You can like your house or car, but you are not your house or car. For instance, I had a black Porsche 911, and I loved that car. Unfortunately, business in the office went down, and I had to sell that car. It hurt but I got over it. What did Job say? *The Lord [gives], and the Lord [takes] away; blessed be the name of the Lord* (Job 1: 21b).

Friend, do not worry. God loved you before you had the gourd. God loved you before you had all those material things. Just as God caused that gourd to grow for you, God can cause another gourd to grow. In fact, I believe when God takes those material things from you, it is because God is making room to really bless you. Remember, God said in Malachi 3:10b, *[Put me to the test]… if I will not open you the windows of heaven, and pour you out a blessing, that there shall not be room enough to receive it.*

God loves you, and God created you. Thus, you do have value. Even without the gourd, even without those comfortable things, you do have value. In God's sight, you are precious.

You are fearfully and wonderfully made. You are so important that God has taken the time to number every hair on your head. Therefore, do not concern yourself with the gourd. Concern yourself with the One Who gave you the gourd. And if you stay close to Him, He will bless you again and again and again.

ANGER IS ONLY THE BEGINNING

So, we see in verse 9 of our text that Jonah still had not calmed down. *And God said to Jonah, Doest thou well to be angry for the gourd? And he said, I do well to be angry, even unto death.* Can you believe it? Jonah was still angry and his anger appeared to be getting worse. The truth is anger is an emotion that tends to build. Angry people can work their anger up and become madder and madder. If fed, anger can act like a lit match turned upside down: It will burn hot and fast.

Still worse, angry people often lash out at those closest to them. Admit it; you have experienced this. Your boss said something to you, which you did not like, or something upsetting happened to you at work. You could not do anything about it there, so you held your tongue. But, once you got home, the first little thing your spouse or kids did wrong, you became angry and upset at them. You actually were overreacting to what your loved ones did because of what happened between you and someone else at work.

In verse 9 of the text, we see that God was speaking calmly and patiently to Jonah, ***Doest thou well to be angry for the gourd?*** But Jonah was flying off the handle. He was losing his cool, becoming increasingly angry, and becoming more extreme in his responses. As it turns out, anger has several stages of manifestation.

The first stage of anger is mild irritation or discomfort. This usually occurs as a slight upset caused by someone or something. For instance, one of your kids spills red juice on your white shirt. Or, your wife wants to talk to you just as the star basketball player heaves a potential buzzer-beating shot. Or maybe, someone bumps into you at the mall, and your ice cream falls on the floor. The typical response to these minor irritations is, "Aw, forget about it. It's no problem. …No big deal." On the other hand, if left unchecked, this initial stage of anger can progress from mild irritation to indignation.

Indignation, anger's second stage, is the feeling that something must be done, that there must be a righting or avenging of that which is wrong. An indignant response to an upsetting situation normally presents itself as hostility. However, indignation may still go unexpressed. For example, you mutter under your breath or think to yourself about what you would, could, or should do to get back at someone, but you keep it to yourself: "What did they just say? He (or she) does not know who he is messing with. He is just lucky I am saved [at work, in my new suit, in front of my kids, etc.]; otherwise, I would have to show him the real me." But, if you persist in mulling over the upsetting incident, then your indignation will advance into wrath.

Unlike indignation, wrath, anger's third phase, never goes unexpressed. Wrath is described as the strong desire to avenge what is wrong. Wrath manifests as a person cursing, screaming, yelling, slamming doors, and breaking things. But, believe it or not, one's anger can burn even hotter than wrath.

Anger can burn to the point of fury, which is the fourth level of the emotion. Fury, also known as rage, presents as a loss of emotional control. Unfortunately, rage or fury often leads to violence. Rage occurs when a person says, "I am going to kill you or myself," and the person really means it. Police statistics report that eighty percent of all murders are committed by someone the victim knew. Sadly, the majority of all murders are typically committed by the victim's spouse or lover. After all, who else can make a person so angry as to want to commit murder?

So, we see in verse 9 as Jonah argued with God, he appeared to be furious. After all, he had attempted to run away from God's presence and assignment for him, only to get caught. Recall that Jonah paid the fare to board a cargo ship and went to sleep. Due to a terrible storm, the ship's captain woke him up. For some people, just being awakened suddenly is enough to make them angry or irritated.

But, then, after a period of questions and debate, the sailors threw Jonah overboard. That meant Jonah wasted the money he had paid for the ship and did not reach his desired destination of Tarshish. Nobody likes to pay for a trip and have it cancelled, let alone to be thrown overboard in the middle of a terrible storm. Jonah thought he was going to drown in the sea. I can imagine he threatened to write the cruise line or shipping company to complain about the terrible conditions and outrageous service he had received. He probably demanded his money back or for his next trip to be free.

And dare we forget, Jonah was swallowed by a great fish and trapped in its belly for three whole days? For three whole days, he was trapped and tangled in seaweed with nothing to read and no television. He had planned to travel first class; instead, he was traveling no class. After all that, the fish had the nerve to vomit him up onto shore. Thus, Jonah did not receive the typical pleasant "goodbye" from the cruise staff. Rather, he received a *"get out and stay out"*.

To make matters worse, Jonah was forced to preach to Nineveh, a city of Gentiles and total strangers. What fun is that? He likely thought, "Nobody knows me there, and I know they are not going to like what I have to say. And just why do I have to preach to them anyway? All of the other prophets, like Isaiah, Daniel, and that crybaby, Jeremiah, get to preach to our brethren of Israel. But, do I? N-o-o-o-o-o. I have to be the first prophet to preach to the Gentiles. It's so unfair!"

On top of all of that, after Jonah delivered his sermon to the people of Nineveh and they repented, he likely said, "God has the nerve to forgive them. That makes me look like a fool, like a foolish false prophet. That's the reason I ran away in the first place: I knew God was going to forgive Nineveh. So, why make me preach to them? That is exactly why, when I finished my sermon, I just left the city because I wanted to see what would become of it. But, when a gourd grew to protect me from the weather, a worm attacked it and it shriveled up. Now, here I am suffering until I faint from the heat of the day or freeze from the cold of the night. And you ask me, *Doest [I] well to be angry for the gourd? … [Yes], I do well to be angry, even unto death* (Jonah 4:9)!"

It is quite apparent by the tone he took with God that Jonah had gradually worked his way through all the stages of anger until he had reached the point of rage. Jonah was actually furious to the point that he wanted someone to pay. Either Nineveh had to die, or he did! It is true, his logic sounded completely childish, selfish, and just plain crazy. But his rationale, conversation, and behavior were typical of someone enraged.

Jonah's display of fury fits the pattern of someone who may be feeling unappreciated at work or at home, for example. Frustration has been steadily building without any hope of remedying the situation. Finally, the day comes when the person snaps and, seemingly without warning, explodes on anyone in his or her path.

A SOFT ANSWER

The funny thing about anger is, sometimes, if the angry party is left to vent, he (or she) will burn and fizzle out, just like that lit match if left all alone and untouched. Face facts, it is hard to carry on an argument when no one will fight you back. And it is unsatisfying to argue, fuss, and fight when the one you are hostile toward responds to you in a manner which is cool, calm, and collected.

God provided us with the cure for anger in Proverbs 15:1: *A soft answer [turns] away wrath*. Additionally, God demonstrated the perfect application of anger's cure by how serenely He spoke to Jonah. God was firm with Jonah but, at the same time, He was gentle with him, speaking the truth in love. Jonah 4:10-11 reads, *Then said the Lord, Thou hast had pity on the gourd, for the which thou hast not labored, neither madest it grow; which came up in a night, and perished in a night: And should not I spare Nineveh, that great city, wherein are more than sixscore thousand persons that cannot discern between their right hand and their left hand; and also much cattle?*

In a perfectly peaceful manner, God pointed out how Jonah had pitied a plant, which he had neither seeded nor nourished nor watered. All the plant had done was supply him with temporal relief and shade, and he wished not to see it wither. Yet, Jonah refused to understand why God would pity an entire city *wherein [the population was] more than sixscore thousand [or 120,000] persons that cannot discern between their right hand and their left hand; and also much cattle* (Jonah 4:11b). Only babies or infants do not know the difference between right and wrong. Since the city contained 120,000 of them, there would have resided in Nineveh several times more adults, teens, and children, besides numerous cattle – all of whom repented, fasted, and turned from their evil ways.

The gourd was a large leafy weed, which sprung up over night. Nineveh, on the other hand was a large populated city, rich with ancient history. Therefore, although Jonah said he did well to be angry, he could not rationalize his anger. He could not justify wanting all of those people, babies, and cattle to die. On the other hand, God could justify desiring to spare all of those precious lives.

Aren't you so glad God is so patient, merciful, and kind that He desires not to see anyone lost? Even if others do not worship, look, act, or dress like you, God cares for them, He loves them, and He wants to save them. Therefore, do not be angry with others or God when things do not go your way. Rather, listen to what God has to say. James 1:19 instructs us to ...*be swift to hear, slow to speak, slow to wrath*. Did you ever stop to think that God gave us two ears and one mouth, so we could listen more and talk less?

One of the best ways not to become angry when things do not go your way is to maintain a good sense of humor. My mother always says, "Turn life's lemons into lemonade." Oftentimes, when you change your attitude, God rewards you with a delightful experience. However, the choice is yours. You may choose to be offended whenever things do not go your way and constantly live on the edge of anger, which is one letter away from "danger". Or, you may make the wise decision to learn to overlook offenses and live a much more   peaceable   life.

Learn to take your cue from Ephesians 4:26-32, which begins… *Be ye angry, and sin not*: Sure you get angry. We all do. Anger is a natural human emotion. Stuff happens and people disappoint you. If you can love, you can get angry. The key is – in your anger, do not sin. Do not let anger build up in you to the point that you lose control and wish to harm someone else or yourself because that is sin.

The "b" clause of Ephesians 4:26 continues, *Let not the sun go down upon your wrath:* Whatever you do, do not let your anger boil, build, or fester overnight. For, verse 27 warns *…neither give, place to the devil*. As we have discussed, anger unleashed easily becomes an avenue to bad behavior, bad speech, revenge, and malicious actions. Anger which festers is like deadly, contagious poison: It affects all who come in contact with it, and anyone who is exposed to it long enough will eventually display its revolting symptoms. Rather *…as much as lieth in you, live peaceably with all men* (Romans 12:18), and speak the truth to them in love. And if the one you are speaking to will not receive what you have to say, it is okay to bow out of the discussion. After all, is being right always that important?

Moreover, Ephesians 4:26-32 states in verse 29a, *Let no corrupt communication proceed out of your mouth.* Do not be like Jonah hoping for the death of others or yourself. Instead, take your example from Jesus and speak life – *that which is good to the use of edifying, that it may minister grace unto the hearers* (verse 29b). God knows what we have need of before we even ask Him, so there is no need to remain in anger. What God has for you is for you. Even if people lie about you, talk about you, or mistreat you, do not make matters worse. Just trust the Lord God to deliver you in His own time and to grace you with wisdom and patience. Things will not stay as they are; it is God's will for you to walk in victory.

Finally, let us examine verses 31 and 32, which read, *Let all bitterness, and wrath, and anger, and clamor, and evil speaking, be put away from you, with all malice: And be ye kind one to another, tenderhearted, forgiving one another, even as God for Christ's sake hath forgiven you.* Remember to treat others with kindness and tenderness of heart. Pursue peace with others by not being easily offended. And endeavor to see the viewpoint of others because yours is not the only opinion that matters. By all means, learn to forgive because everyone (even you) makes mistakes.

Just remember the "Lord's prayer": ***forgive us our sins; for we also forgive everyone that is indebted to us*** (Luke 11:2-4). Thankfully, God forgave you, so surely you can forgive others. And when in doubt of what to do or how to behave, show love, just as you would want God, the Heavenly Father, to show love toward you.

Epilogue

I decided to end this book with an epilogue because Jonah's emotional journey had no real conclusion. In fact, several people have told me they did not like the end of the *Book of Jonah* since he never seemed to learn his lesson. After Jonah fainted and said, "It is better for me to die than to live," Jonah never spoke again, though the Lord spoke, chastising him for having more concern for a gourd than for the population of nearly one million souls in Nineveh.

A peaceful response assuages wrath. Although the Lord corrected Jonah, He did so with calm and kindness. Therefore, I believe that Jonah's anger was quieted. However, there is no indication that Jonah ever changed his mind. Quite possibly, Jonah saw the salvation of Nineveh as an entirely negative event; then, he spoke with the Lord and went on his way still feeling disappointed.

For those of us who struggle with emotions as did Jonah, there are times when we do not receive victory or calm the stormy seas of our sentiments. How many of us can recall things that happened over ten, twenty, or even thirty years ago, and we still become upset, almost as if it occurred just yesterday?

Yet, there is hope that we can do and be better, for the Lord takes us from faith to faith and from glory to glory. It is true, many of us, like Jonah, have been drifting from embarrassment to guilt to depression to grief to anger. Yes, it does seem, after we pass one test, that we are carried on to the next. And, when we do not learn to control our emotions at a particular level, we remained docked at that emotional port.

Still, I have a future hope and expectation for us all. Our experiences, and that of Jonah's, teach us that God is always with us. Even when we let our emotions get the better of us, even when we allow our judgment to become clouded, and even when we disobey God, He yet is preparing something for us. God may not have huge fish or gourds prepared for us; however, I am convinced that He has prepared something for us. And He is perfecting those things –including our emotions – which concern us.

Whether a job, a house, a mate, children, health, or wealth, I know there is something that the Lord has prepared for you. I am certain of this because God loves you. Even when you are at your worst, God still loves you. And He is moving and working on your behalf if you love and follow Him. Remember, in the midst of your emotional storm, when you feel all alone, be encouraged. Just as God was with Jonah, preparing and providing for him along his way, He also will be with you as you continue your life's emotional journey......

www.ingramcontent.com/pod-product-compliance
Lightning Source LLC
Chambersburg PA
CBHW032117040426
42449CB00005B/175